Inevitable/Human - Volume 1

Inevitable/Human - Volume 1

Essays on Emerging Technology That Will Change Our Future

QUHARRISON TERRY AND RYAN COWDREY

VICTORY IS NEVER MERCILESS, LLC.
MADISON, WI

Contents

Introduction

Inevitable/Human is a futuristic newsletter and online support network for Futurists, Technologists, and Business Professionals who want to anticipate the future and foresee transformative changes. We publish exclusive content on emerging technology and other Future(s) Studies concepts to spark conversation among our community members.

Our community spans five continents, encompasses a plethora of backgrounds, and brings together vastly different perspectives of technological change. However, one thing remains consistent across each member – the desire to enhance their strategic foresight and better understand the future that's unfolding before them.

This volume is a collection of essays based on emerging technologies and concepts we found intriguing from the end of 2017 to late 2018. Each essay provides readers with an in-depth analysis of a technology trend and presents a future application of the technology while keeping the information easily accessible to everyone. The essays vary in length and are presented as they appear on the Inevitable/Human website. Although we've curated the order for flow, it is important to note that we didn't design this to be read sequentially and readers can browse the essays in any order they wish.

1. The fax machine: A technological anomaly

"Imagine a world without fax machines", is a talking point you've probably never encountered. Wedged somewhere in the timeline between the telephone and the personal computer, fax machines are a technology afterthought and are almost never referenced as an influential 20th-century technology among the ranks of the automobile, the radio, and the computer.

However, fax machines were an essential step in forming current communication behaviors. Without fax machines, we might not have been as open to the idea of email and instant messaging. Without fax machines, the personal computer (and thus the smartphone) may not have been well received.

The year is nearing 2019 and the fax machine has managed to survive in hospitals, law offices, and homes worldwide. However, 2020 will be the year we finally begin digging the fax machine's grave where it will lay for eternity.

> In July 2018, a Freedom of Information request (FOI) revealed that over 8,000 fax machines were being used by the NHS. This week, MP Matt Hancock, Health and Social Care Secretary, announced that from 2020 all fax machines in the NHS will be phased out, with a ban in place to stop trusts purchasing them.
> – Phee Waterfield, Forbes

There's never been a better time to do a retrospective on the fax machine. To recognize the uncanny influence it had on the computer and smartphone. To credit it with playing a role in shaping the behaviors of the Information Age. And ultimately, analyze its life in hopes that it can inform us of the solution to one of humanity's most pressing plagues: device addiction.

The Life of Fax

Pre-internet, the fax machine was a convenient and swift way to send large amounts of information at a distance. Every office worldwide and a vast majority of homes used this unsexy piece of technology to communicate.

One of the early use cases of facsimile (fax), was delivering the news. Faxpapers were sent via radio waves, which consumers could then tune the dial on their radiofax printing machine to print the daily newspaper. Although it only ever caught on with a dozen or so newspapers in the 1930s and 1940s, faxpapers were our first foray into instant news. Unfortunately for faxpapers, the television would prove to be a more effective platform for real-time news.

But, facsimile didn't die in the 40s. The Xerox Corporation revived it in the mid-1960s by replacing radio transmission with telephone transmission. This was a defining moment in fax machine history because it allowed anyone with a telephone landline to hook up to a fax machine.

Flash forward a couple decades to the 1980s and the commercial fax machine is in its heyday. It became the go-to device to send memos, reports, and private info. But, it was more than a single function tool. It was a platform that allowed faxers to experiment with different communication experiences.

One Manhattan restaurant, Piatti Pronti, created Lunch by Fax which allowed hungry faxers to send their lunch order to the restaurant via fax. Lunch by Fax was a more accurate order system than phoning into a restaurant, as their business went up 10% thanks to the idea. In many ways, Lunch by Fax was the first version of GrubHub and EatStreet, which are today's standard in online food ordering. Fax machines were first to enhance the food ordering service.

Faxpapers made a small comeback for the Connecticut newspaper, The Hartford Courant. Learning from the early faxpaper mistakes, they created a subscription faxpaper service that delivered a one-page summary of the next day's morning newspaper. 100s of businesses in the Hartford area subscribed to gain this small competitive advantage.

In a 1990 article titled, *Overwhelmed with Fax Attacks*, the Washington Post talked with faxers that were using their fax machines to send in song requests to the local radio station. Some used the machine to send a friend their birthday card or a funny comic strip (sounds a little like early social media). For the procrastinating type, fax machines provided a great opportunity to organize football betting pools while the boss wasn't looking. Even solicitors were using fax machines to send people Junk Faxes.

Later in the article, the Post described the reasons for the fax sensation, "...fax is cheaper, easier and faster than other forms of staying in touch. The mail takes days; a courier takes hours and costs dearly. Fax moves in seconds. Unlike a phone conversation, it can convey pictures, charts, graphics, doodles, handwriting. Unlike telephone calls, it leaves a record."

It's not hard to understand why fax was such a hit throughout the 80s and 90s – reaching peak sales of 3.6 million fax machines sold in 1997. However, the tool hasn't lasted in the popular mass. Today, the multi-purpose fax machine is present in a meager 18.7% of U.S. citizens' lives. Compare this to the mobile phone, which 86.3% of the U.S. population owns, and you see that the fax machine just isn't a major tool anymore. Outside of lawyers and doctors faxing signed documents, you'd be hard-pressed to find an active "faxer". Faxing has become an innovation afterthought in nearly every facet of our lives.

So, why did we cast this piece of technology away like we do our empty coffee cups?

Natural Cycle of Progress

Well, for the same reasons that fax gained popularity, is why fax eventually died. Email proved to be a communication tool that was cheaper, easier, and faster. To this day, chain emails entertain us. Email newsletters inform us. Sales emails advertise to us. Email provided people with many of the same experiences as the fax machine except on a better platform, the personal computer. And thus goes the cycle of emerging technology.

Even though the fax machine's time in the spotlight was short-lived, that doesn't mean we can't learn anything from its existence. In fact, the fax machine's rise to popularity was centered on two simple truths – it was fun and easy.

There was something magical about dialing a phone number and sending a piece of paper so easily. And when you heard those distinct "sending tones", you knew that your fax had worked and a little burst of dopamine rushed throughout your brain. I remember the first time I saw my mom receive a fax. I was mesmerized by this mysterious event. Where did this come from? Who was on the other end? Why was my mom chosen?

In a time when personal computers were complex and required hours of training, the fax machine was the cool older brother that everyone wanted to be around. It was slick and simple. And that's why it caught on.

Smartphones: A Societal Crutch

When you think about intuitive technologies of today, you cannot pass over the smartphone. As if it took lessons from its grandparent (the fax machine), the smartphone is easier, faster, and more fun to use than the personal computer that came before it.

However, unlike the fax machine and the personal computer, the smartphone has created a moat that will make it very hard to be replaced. The smartphone has brought together dozens of devices into one tool. The GPS, MP3 player, calculator, handheld gaming device, alarm clock, kitchen timer, calendar, and many more are all irrelevant devices thanks to the smartphone. Although combining all these devices into one has made the smartphone one of the most convenient tools available, it's brought with it a set of consequences.

You cannot deny that we are addicted to our smartphones. Ten years ago, losing a cell phone wasn't a big deal. You probably had many phone numbers memorized and could just borrow someone else's if you needed to make a call. Today, losing your cell phone means losing access to your lifestyle – emails about work updates, alerts between family and friends, and even your entertainment through social media, games, and videos. The smartphone is an extension of our being. Without it, it seems as though we cannot "be".

Contrast this against the fax machine, who nobody was behaviorally attached to. The smartphone addiction tells us a lot about our behaviors.

Not only is the smartphone act as the door to the rest of the world, but it's becoming a societal crutch. In the same way that my grandfather's generation turned to martinis and cocktails as a societal crutch, we are turning to the smartphone.

Our smartphones provide comfort and protection from all of life's trials. But, it's a pseudo-comfort and pseudo-protection. As we know about alcohol as a crutch, it's artificial. The smartphone crutch shields us from pain, embarrassment, and loneliness. Instead of professing our identities and opinions in person, we save ourselves the chance of embarrassment by hiding behind our digital voice.

I have many friends that cannot stand the deep feelings of loneliness that surface before bedtime, so they fall asleep to the glow of their Facebook feed for distraction.

When situations are awkward, boring, or nerve-wracking out come the smartphones. Go to a bar and notice how many people are wrapped in their phone, instead of interacting with strangers. The same goes for the boring bus or train ride to work. Who's actually embracing life's banal situations to inspire them to meet new people?

Just like the popular crutch of the 20th century, the smartphone as a crutch is very dangerous. An alcohol hangover resurfaces whatever we tried to escape with drunkenness. The smartphone hangover amplifies our problems by disconnecting us from our own emotions.

Smartphones are putting silence out of business and it's in silence and solitude where we have those tough conversations with ourselves. How can you expect to "follow your heart", "find your passion", or "know yourself" if every time your heart tries to talk about your problems you turn to a screen?

Our emotions make us real and blocking those feelings with a smartphone distraction makes you more artificial.

Finding Harmony

I'm not proposing we kill the smartphone. On the contrary, I think it's a fantastic tool to use. The problem is that many of us allow the smartphone to use us. They allow Facebook to use hours of their attention for profit – distracted from personal progress. They allow Candy Crush to steal time from interacting with friends.

It's imperative that we realize the gravity of this situation. The rush of dopamine our brains receive a couple hundred times a day from the phone's vibration in our pockets will have serious effects on us. The medical field has already recognized Phantom Vibration Syndrome – a condition where we perceive our phones to be ringing/vibrating when they really aren't. In other words, we crave the feeling of being pinged so badly that our brains will literally hallucinate a notification. This should be a major warning sign. Michelle Drouin, a researcher that studies the psychological effects of social media and communications technology, found that 9 out of 10 undergraduates at her college experienced phantom vibrations. And I would bet a large portion of smartphone users have experienced a phantom vibration (I know I have).

Anyways, I draw the parallel to smartphone's forefather, the fax machine because people used the fax machine in many of the same ways we use our smartphones – to communicate and connect. But, using the fax machine didn't take away from our human identity. It didn't replace our ability to connect with others or even ourselves.

We cannot expect to grow as individuals if we continue to rely on the smartphone as a societal crutch. The trend I would like to see going forward into 2019, is an honest search from everyone to find a personal harmony between their technology and healthy, productive behaviors.

We're beginning to notice the Zeitgeist flowing in a positive direction. I'm hearing more and more people around me complain about their almost unconscious technology addiction, which means there's a desire to make a change.

Just in the past few years, the term "digital detox" has grown as a topic of discussion. Camp Grounded – a digital detox camp for adults – was way ahead of its time opening in 2013. Today, there are dozens of these camps for kids and adults to help them beat internet addictions and disconnect from the digital livelihood.

On a larger scale, Vitamin Water just launched a competition called the Scroll-Free Challenge that will award up to $100,000 to anyone that can spend all 365 days of 2019 without using their smartphone.

Although the logistics of the challenge don't quite add up (how will you prove that you didn't use your phone), it's still great to see the people and brands with a voice putting this great message out there.

Even legislators are getting involved. Earlier this year, a New York Senator proposed a bill called The Right To Disconnect which proposed a human right regarding the ability of people to disconnect from work and primarily not to engage in work-related electronic communications such as e-mails or messages during non-work hours.

A YouTube element has been excluded from this version of the text. You can view it online here:
https://qtv1.pressbooks.com/?p=289

Even though there are small pockets of change occurring, this is no time to rest on our laurels. It's an active change that must happen within us all.

We must strive for a symbiotic relationship between technology and humanity. When one overpowers the other, we lose something precious. Too much human-centeredness and we lose progress. Too much technology and we lose our humanity.

2. Google may soon know the day you'll die

Google built a hundred-billion-dollar behemoth by giving us answers to all of our questions. Now, they may be able to give us an answer to the most worrisome question of all: When will I die?

Predicting the Inevitable

In some way or another, we've all learned from the deceased. Whether it's the family stories passed down about your ambitious grandmother. Or the wisdom found in a passing quote. Part of our duty as human beings is to learn from those that came before.

And that includes Google as well, who is learning from the deceased. Not how to live a better life. But rather the patterns that lead up to death.

Essentially, they're training an algorithm that can predict a patient's length of stay, time of discharge, and maybe even their time of death. For it to be accurate, the algorithm requires thousands of electronic health records including patient demographics, provider orders, diagnoses, procedures, medications, laboratory values, vital signs, and flowsheet data.

Ideally, understanding the patterns of how people's bodies may react under similar circumstances could be the "saving grace" for the nearly 750,000 people(in America) who die in hospitals every year.

This algorithm could help hospitals better allocate resources to those that may be on the verge of critical needs and preparing staff for problems before they occur.

The fact that Google is spearheading this technology is definitely cause for concern. We're already aware of the insane power they yield. Predicting lifespan would bring their company to oracular proportions.

This makes me think of the manga series, Death Note, which follows a teen who stumbles upon a notebook with unprecedented power –

write any name in the notebook and that person will die. While at first he's driven by the desire to rid the world of all evil. Eventually, the death gods (Shinigami) offer a proposition – in exchange for half of his life, the Shinigami give him their eyes which can identify the name and remaining lifespan of anyone he looks at.

This is the same corruptive power that Google could potentially wield and that is quite worrisome.

Imagine how their services would change if they knew when anyone using their search engine was going to die. Would they hint at your demise and try to change your behaviors? What types of services would they try to sell us?

I think the majority of us wouldn't have any interest in knowing the exact day or year of our death (if it were possible). However, if there were a way to procrastinate our deaths, I'm sure the response would be a little different.

Life Extension

Ever since Juan Ponce de Leon navigated the tropical Florida waters, a myth arose about a mystical Fountain of Youth. A place where wrinkles vanished and people lived in their youthful glory for eternity.

While the Fountain of Youth has inspired storytellers for centuries, it is actually the scientists of today that are gaining inspiration from this tale.

Aubrey de Grey is one of these men who believe that there's a cure for aging. Based on his theories that cells encounter seven types of aging damage(mutations, junk, etc...), he believes the science already exists to create anti-aging medicine – ideally making 90 the new 50 in the next decade. That's why he co-founded the SENS Research Foundation and Methuselah Foundation to bring great minds (and great wealth) to the field of tissue engineering and regenerative medicine therapies.

Then there's the billionaire fashion mogul, Peter Nygard, who's been injecting himself with stem cells for years – claiming that his team of scientists is reversing the aging process (many critics are skeptical).

Stem cells are undoubtedly a possible form of rejuvenation. They are unique in that they are undifferentiated; they can become anything, like a blank canvas. So the possibility of using them to regenerate damaged tissues, nerves, etc... is an optimistic dream.

Taking a different approach to immortality is Eternime – a company that will create a digital replica of you (from your social media and text messages) after you've passed away so that your family can interact with a chatbot that talks just like you. Although this form of digital immortality does nothing to prevent death. It does prolong the memories made on Earth, which are valuable in another way.

Then again, if we can't find the keys to immortality today, there's always Cryonics (Cryogenics), which is the process of preserving body and mind in freezing temperatures to be revived at a later date.

In the movie *Vanilla Sky*, for example, David Aames is in a near-fatal car accident that disfigures his face, leaving the bachelor in absolute despair. Facial reconstruction surgery cannot fix his face, so he decides to be cryogenically frozen until the surgery is advanced. Things are great until his subconscious begins fighting with him, confusion of reality and the lucid dream state sets in, and the psychological thriller unfolds.

"Something tells me he's gonna wish he remained frozen"

Personally, I find Cryonics a bit comical because it exists on the notion that in the future, once science has found cures for aging and other diseases, someone you've never met will bring you back from your frozen state. This means that Cryonics companies today are literally getting rich on Hope.

Although there seem to be a few different strategies for attaining life extension goals. They are all united in common belief: death and aging are just another problem to solve.

Existential Breakthrough

Aubrey de Grey coined the term "pro-aging trance", which is the impulsion to leap to embarrassingly unjustified conclusions in order to put the horror of aging out of one's mind. In other words, it's the common belief that aging is just a part of life and there's nothing we could nor should do about it.

De Grey and other proponents believe that the pro-aging trance is the largest barrier to life extension progress, considering it's a wide-held cultural belief. Nonetheless, it's not stopping them from continuing research and pushing the envelope.

While at the moment, early anti-aging methods may be reserved for lab rats and eccentric billionaires. There will come a time when the public is given the opportunity to postpone the physical and cognitive deterioration we've come to accept as part of growing old.

In fact, I believe that in 25 years, just one generation from now, scientists will have conquered aging – giving us the chance to extend our lives by decades.

Follow Your Bliss

I've said it before when covering technological immortality. I don't know which I fear more: Dying before I've accomplished all my dreams or living past the point of enjoying life.

For that reason, it's best to take every day as it comes – treat it as a gift and follow your bliss.

If a day goes by where you aren't working toward something that brings you joy, then it's time to change your course.

If scientists conquer aging, then one day we may say, "Life is too long." But for now, life is too short to not spend each day following your bliss.

3. The Data Factories and Virtual Sweatshops that make the Internet run smoothly

If history class taught me anything about the Industrial Revolution, it was that the regulations on working conditions were non-existent. No age limit. No hour limit. No minimum wage. Factory jobs were not sweet, but if it was your only way to survive, then you accepted it.

Unfortunately, it appears that history is repeating itself.

Hundreds of thousands of people are finding themselves in this exact same position, except with a digital twist. The amount of legal ambiguity in the data industry is absurd. Thus, we have unregulated, virtual sweatshops of the Internet.

Data Factories

The largest constraint to improving artificial intelligence is obtaining a quality stream of data that is useful to the given algorithm. In other words, artificial intelligence doesn't know what it doesn't know. And it's up to humans to tell it what it needs to know.

For something as seemingly simple to us humans as identifying road signs, this equates to tens of millions of labeled images (containing the numerous visual scenarios) needed in order for the algorithm to successfully identify a sign. That's a lot of annotated photographs, which is why there's an entire economy around purifying and preparing data for AI.

Mechanical Turk is one of these websites that offer people pennies to tag photos, complete surveys, and other HITs (Human Intelligence Tasks) that'll help AI systems learn. Companies such as Twitter,

LinkedIn, Dropbox, DARPA, will put their tasks on Mechanical Turk at insanely cheap labor rates.

Ars Technica did an exposé on the lifestyles of Mechanical Turk workers, and it's just horrendous. We're talking about completing hundreds or thousands of these micro-tasks daily just to scrape together around $6.50 per hour. It really is the assembly line of the 21st century. And there's no regulation:

> The tasks that pay the best and take the least time get snapped up quickly by workers, so Erica must monitor the site closely, waiting to grab them. She doesn't get paid for that time looking, or for the time she spends, say, getting a glass of water or going to the bathroom. Sometimes, she has to "return" tasks—which means sending them back to the requester, usually because the directions are unclear—after she's already spent precious time on them.
>
> **ALANA SEMUELS,** THE ATLANTIC

It's really a bad situation for the workers in the developed world where the cost of living far exceeds what they can earn. This is why companies like Samasource outsource some of these data prep jobs to places like Kenya, where a few dollars a day is a somewhat respectable wage.

Another role that falls into this Data Factory category, and perhaps the worst part of the Internet's underbelly, is content moderation.

The Internet Cleaners

The Cleaners is a PBS documentary about the thousands of Internet and social media content moderators that clean up the graphic junk that pollute the Internet. Beheadings, sexual abuse, hate crimes, child exploitation, terror threats – these are horrible things that we never have to come across in our daily searches thanks to these moderators that remove them.

As if the graphic nature of the job weren't enough, they must review 25,000 pictures a day just to meet their requirements. If they're working eight hour days (which I highly doubt), that equates to reviewing an image/video every 1.15 seconds. For a twelve hour work day, that's an image every 1.72 seconds. They are literally tasked with moderating free speech in the free world in mere seconds. That's a lot of responsibility.

Not to mention the horrible repercussions. Imagine seeing violent crimes and disturbing images of children every day for six straight years. That'll change you as a person. It's truly a selfless job that benefits the whole while weakening the few.

Whether you're tagging images, moderating content, taking surveys, these are the Data Factories of the 21st century. They are unregulated, ridden with horrible working conditions, and necessary for the functioning of digital society.

Our dependence on data is not slowing down anytime soon. We've only seen great penetration in the technologically savvy companies and already millions of people work in data handling. Clickworker, another one of these micro-tasking companies, claims 1.3 million clickworkers. That's just one of many platforms providing these micro-tasks.

In rural towns where the economies are stricken, in overpopulated cities where the opportunities are scarce, people with few options to earn a living will continue filing into these Data Factories.

It's hard not to be angry at this outlook. It's hard not to lose sleep over this livelihood. That's why it's best to be thankful for their contribution to making your life better.

4. YouTube and Netflix algorithms are slaves to your time

"The greatest trick the devil ever pulled was convincing the world he didn't exist", *The Usual Suspects*. Today, artificial intelligence is following the basis of this quote. Although not very devilish in its ways, AI has done an incredible job convincing the world it doesn't exist. Most of us consumers simply don't realize when AI is working its magic.

Where are the brands in AI?

We have countless software brands: Gmail, Facebook, Salesforce, Netflix, Uber, Robinhood, Spotify, Snapchat, Maps, etc… And each of these use AI in a plethora of ways.

> Consumers, however, have few ways to understand when and how AI is being used, and to judge for themselves if they see it as a benefit or not. It's simply not a recognizable element of a brand. If AI is to become a meaningful facet of society, identifiable and understandable by consumers, its value must be articulated. And for that to happen, designers of AI-driven experiences must make the invisible visible; they have to give AI a good, old-fashioned brand identity.
>
> The key obstacle that AI faces, from a branding perspective, is that it has been engineered to be invisible. AI is often deployed as a way to eliminate friction and to reduce people's awareness of technology. Unlike other familiar brand elements – color, typography, logos, texture, sound, tone of voice, photography style – AI is often seen as being most successful when it's completely invisible.
>
> **JASON BRUSH,** FAST COMPANY

This invisibility of AI is, in some cases, a benefit to the user and in other cases a detriment. Take, for example, the difference between Netflix and YouTube.

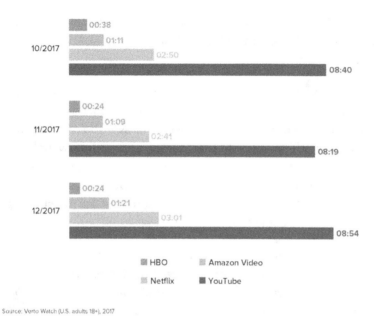

Time Spent per User (hours:minutes) on Leading Video Streaming Services

10/2017	HBO	00:38	
	Amazon Video	01:11	
	Netflix	02:50	
	YouTube	08:40	
11/2017	HBO	00:24	
	Amazon Video	01:09	
	Netflix	02:41	
	YouTube	08:19	
12/2017	HBO	00:24	
	Amazon Video	01:21	
	Netflix	03:01	
	YouTube	08:54	

■ HBO ▓ Amazon Video
▒ Netflix ■ YouTube

Source: Verto Watch (U.S. adults 18+), 2017

In December 2017, consumers in the United States spent an average of almost 9 hrs watching YouTube and just over 3 hrs watching Netflix.

Netflix AI vs. YouTube AI

Both Netflix and YouTube invisibly employ AI to deliver your content, but with different effects. Netflix's AI is designed to make the viewing experience simpler. Whereas YouTube's is designed to elongate this viewing experience. And this makes all the difference when it comes to the branding of their AI. Let me explain.

Netflix uses AI to recommend content and convince you to watch their content as quickly as possible. Ideally, their first recommendation works and then the AI is out of the picture while you watch a 90-minute movie. Because Netflix is a subscription service, the less that their subscribers have to search and interact within their platform the more satisfied they are and the more likely they are to continue their subscribers. In Netflix's case, AI is meant to reduce interaction within their platform. It's this philosophy that has led to these numbers (in Q3 2018):

> Netflix signed up 6.96 million customers in the third quarter, boosting its global total to 137.1 million.
> BLOOMBERG

YouTube, on the other hand, is free to use and must make money from advertisements. Therefore, they use AI to increase user interaction on their platform. Its AI is designed to amplify whatever you click on, giving you an endless stream of only that narrow topic. They want you to follow that AI recommendation for as long as possible, while they reel in the advertisement profits. And it's this AI-led experience that has led to these large numbers from this Q2 2017 earnings call (most current and reliable data we could find):

> YouTube now has over 1.5 billion users. On average, these users spend 60 minutes a day on mobile. But this growth isn't just happening on desktop and mobile. YouTube now gets over 100 million hours of watch time in the living room every day, and that's up 70% in the past year alone.
> *SUNDAR PICHAI, CEO OF ALPHABET*

If you search videos about blue skies, it's going to continue giving you blue sky videos forever – not once mentioning the fact that there are red skies. This is known as the YouTube Rabbit Hole. While it seems inconsequential for the color of the sky, it becomes a real issue when the AI sends you down a rabbit hole conspiracy theories, anti-science propaganda, or disturbing videos:

> Thanks to YouTube's autoplay feature for recommended videos, when users watch one popular disturbing children's video, they're more likely to stumble down an algorithm-powered exploitative video rabbit hole. After BuzzFeed News screened a series of these videos, YouTube began recommending other disturbing videos from popular accounts like ToysToSee.
> *CHARLIE WARZEL,* BUZZFEED NEWS

YouTube's autoplay feature that sends people down rabbit holes can be especially detrimental to young minds who may not have the self-control to leave a bad video stream or don't know to actively search for the other side of a story before they believe something.

Both of the AIs are designed to maximize your entertainment (and potentially minimize your productivity). But, the role the AIs play is a little different. YouTube's AI is a slave to advertisements, while Netflix's AI is a servant to the customer.

5. Who will be the first company to brand their AI algorithms?

Almost all companies using AI are deploying their AIs in an invisible way. Whether it's the automatic playlist generation on Spotify or the suggested route on Google Maps, we as consumers are completely unaware when the AI is operating.

Ignorance is bliss, right? Yes, it is. But that doesn't mean it's necessarily the right thing to do. We cannot continue being left in the dark with these intelligent applications that essentially have the power to control our behaviors.

This is why Jason Brush of Fast Company is calling for AI to get "a good, old-fashioned brand identity". Basically, if consumers knew when AI algorithms were being utilized, then they could differentiate the harmful use cases from the beneficial. And thus take action against specific instances of AI, as opposed to attacking the general umbrella of all artificial intelligence.

Obviously, this will not be a simple undertaking.

YouTube AI vs. Netflix AI

Take for example, Netflix and YouTube, which both use AI-generated recommendations to maximize our entertainment. Both of them hide this use of AI behind well-designed interfaces. And both play a critical role in molding people's beliefs through the content they recommend. But, the way in which they deploy AI is vastly different:

> Netflix's AI is designed to make the viewing experience simpler. Whereas YouTube's AI is designed to elongate this viewing experience.
>
> Netflix uses AI to recommend content and convince you to

watch their content as quickly as possible. Ideally, their first recommendation works and then the AI is out of the picture while you watch a 90-minute movie.

YouTube uses AI to amplify whatever you click on, giving you an endless stream of only that narrow topic. They want you to follow that AI recommendation for as long as possible.
INEVITABLE/HUMAN

Therefore, the way in which their AIs are branded and the way in which we discuss the potential dangers will be different.

Branding AI is not that Easy

To illustrate this point, I'll make the comparison to McDonald's and cigarettes, which are both bad for your health (as Netflix and YouTube both are bad for your productivity). But how we go about telling people about the dangers is vastly different.

As soon as you walk in the door, McDonald's aims to give you your food as quick as possible. They follow up this speedy delivery with food that tastes good (subjectively). The proper way to warn people of the dangers of McDonald's is to attack the tasty (but unhealthy) food, not the speedy delivery. It's why *Fast Food Nation* and *Super Size Me* expose the "food" in "fast food". Not the "fast" in "fast food".

Similarly, Netflix's AI aims to deliver speedily and then follow it up with great content. Therefore, the proper way to warn people of the dangers of Netflix is not to warn them of their recommendation algorithm that wants to help you find great content quickly and then be out of your hair. No, it's to warn people of the content itself.

On the other hand, with cigarettes, the addictive nature and unhealthiness isbaked into the cigarette itself. They are engineered to make you use them as long as possible and to want more – similar to how the very nature of the YouTube recommendation algorithm is addictive. This is why the YouTube rabbit hole is a very real threat to people.

Making the YouTube AI brand visible would actually bring benefit in reducing these "YouTube rabbit holes". Maybe they call out that their

AI is making suggestions, in the same way that cigarette companies must put a Surgeon's General warning label on them. This way, we understand that we're being influenced by AI and can decide whether or not to continue using their recommended videos or start a new search.

The point I'm making here is that the branding of AI is a complicated matter. I don't believe that branding AI is going to be a cut-and-dry process like a Coca-cola or Gillette, where we brand a color, a logo, a tagline, and an emotion... and voila! There's an award-winning brand.

On the surface level, Netflix and YouTube algorithms have very similar functions. But, the way in which we tell people about the dangers (and thus educate about moderation) is vastly different.

For a more concrete vision, I think virtual assistants have really given us a taste of how we may brand artificial intelligence in the future.

Branding Virtual Assistants

Each virtual assistant – Siri, Alexa, Cortana, Watson, and Google Assistant – has taken on a name, a recognizable voice, and a slight persona. This branding of the virtual assistants turned the intangible nature of AI into something tangible.

Furthermore, it differentiates the options. With virtual assistants, it's now about choosing sides. People see Siri as unhelpful, so they don't rock with that brand. They see Alexa as helpful, so they rock with it.

More specifically, each branded virtual assistant now becomes responsible for their actions. For instance, in my office, when Alexa falsely hears a wake word and interrupts a conversation I'm having, I'm somewhat aware that the voice recognition AI is present and made a mistake. If I'm in the middle of a meeting, I'll turn Alexa off. By branding this AI, the user is aware the AI is operating, and thus, can make decisions if they want to continue using it or not.

Looking to the next five years, as virtual assistants begin entering new mediums (VR in particular), this AI branding can be taken one step further through the use of digital humans. A prime example is how Cortana (Microsoft's virtual assistant) took on a digital human form in *Halo 4*.

Isn't it possible that YouTube could employ a digital human on their website that informs people of the AI in use. Or, as is the case with Cortana in *Halo*, the digital human is the AI – thus, the digital human is the AI's brand. I elaborate a bit more on this concept of digital humans being present in our software in the Quick Theories: How Domino's is leading us into the era of conversational interfaces.

The fact that AI applications are brandless, invisible, and therefore rarely held accountable for their wrongdoing, seems like a minor issue today. This is because, as far as we know, AI is making our lives more efficient, more informed, and more entertained. But, with the flip of a switch, this can be reversed. And then we'll be in deep trouble.

AI is not going to recede from our existence. In fact, we're really just getting started:

> The business plans of the next 10,000 startups are easy to forecast: take X and add AI.
> **KEVIN KELLY,** WIRED

Therefore, as long as we're in the early stages of AI, why don't we create the process for which we can identify AI's role. For society to operate and have a constructive relationship with AI, it's important that we can understand when and how AI is being used, and to judge for ourselves on a case by case basis if we see it as a benefit or not.

6. Why the Fortune 500 desperately needs an AI Board of Directors

Instinct, acumen, and industry foresight. Three crucial components to guiding a brand or corporation through mergers, industry instability, and overall strategy.

When instinct is wrong, you become "the company that made the wrong move" like Kodak. When acumen lacks, you become an afterthought like Dell. When industry foresight is absent, you become obsolete like Blockbuster. Companies who aren't capitalizing will be crumbled.

> **...the cost of bad decisions is high... Consider that 50% of the Fortune 500 companies are forecasted to fall off the list within a decade, and that failure rates are high for new product launches, mergers and acquisitions, and even attempts at digital transformation.**
> **BARRY LIBERT & OTHERS,** MIT SLOAN REVIEW

It's not like folks don't see failure coming. A 2015 McKinsey study found that only 16% of board directors said they fully understood how the dynamics of their industries were changing and how technological advancement would alter the trajectories of their company and industry. Business is moving faster than ever; boards and executives cannot continue to make great decisions without the help of intelligent systems.

We often perceive algorithms to have a great impact on small tasks, but their greatest impact may come in the form of strategic corporate foresight.

Some of the best human strategic thinkers may be able to think five or six moves ahead. But, they can't juggle this same process with dozens or hundreds of decisions at once. On the other hand, one of the main tenets of machine learning algorithms is their ability to run millions of simulations and peruse terabytes of data in a matter of minutes.

Currently, we see this skill being utilized to support capital investment.

> **BlackRock says it relies on it [AI] for heavy cognitive lifting, often by scouring data to tease out patterns that might remain obscure to human eyes and brains. Examples offered by Jessica Greaney, a company spokeswoman, include identifying and trying to exploit nonintuitive relationships between securities or market indicators, perusing social media "to gain insights on employee attitudes, sentiment and preferences," and monitoring search engines for words being entered on particular topics, say cars or luxury goods.**
>
> **CONRAD DE AENLLE,** NY TIMES

These same processes could be tweaked to support corporate executives when building strategy. They might use AI to scan particular industries for emerging competition. Then, running simulations to weigh their likelihood of future success. And possibly even deciding what is the ideal merger & acquisition scenario. This isn't a foolproof plan, though.

> **AI is only as good as the data and resources that you give it. If the AI works off of false assumptions or your organisation has poor data quality, then you could be led astray. The underlying infrastructure and data sources need to be sound before the AI can make meaningful contributions to the company.**
>
> MARK VAN RIJMENAM

AI's reliance on data brings up another question: can AI make accurate predictions where little or no data exists? For instance, if Coca-Cola employed an advanced AI Board Member today, would it have found, assessed, and invested in BodyArmor SuperDrink far earlier and gotten a better deal?

This comes back to the element of instinct. It's hard to predict a skyrocket trend that comes out of nowhere. And by no means is this something that relies solely on a Board of Directors to recognize.

However, ideally, an AI could one day find these trends before they take off.

It's important to note, though, that far sooner on the timeline for AI's role in the workplace will be the commercialization of virtual assistants like Fin.

We know that business relies heavily on relationship building and a human assistant can be an executive's biggest weapon for this task. However, they are often times bogged down by the menial duties such as calendar upkeep, travel coordination, and writing emails. Very soon, virtual assistants will relieve employees of these simpler duties, allowing them to focus full-time on the actions that'll help their boss build better client relationships (remembering small and meaningful details, reading behaviors, giving the perfect gift, etc.).

Although we're beginning to see investment firms employ AI to assist in decision-making, the role is very limited. Similarly, AI will be stuck in a supporting role for quite some time before they are guiding boardroom strategy.

The technology necessary to make sense of something as broad as corporate strategy is quite a ways off. And even then, the implementation curve will be stark.

Around 2038, AI-assisted Board of Directors will begin to be a niche worth watching – with mass adoption coming around 2050.

Nonetheless, an AI-assisted Board of Directors would be worthwhile across a plethora of industries because it theoretically can remove human bias, prevent opportunities from going unnoticed, and ensure resources are being used properly.

7. Everything you need to know about Digital Humans

Photoshop and a little ingenuity are all it takes to create a celebrity these days. I'm not referring to the swaths of Instagram models that have gained notoriety by doctoring all of their photos (although that is a problem we need to discuss later). Rather, I'm referring to digital humans, which are created from scratch. Their stories are fake. Their images are fake. But, their impact is real.

This is a movement that you need to pay attention to. Here's why:

Digital Humans Are Here

Previously, I covered Lil Miquela, the digital human that has gone onto become a digital influencer (with a net worth of $6M) in the fashion industry. But, she's not the first digital human to reach a level of fame.

Many of us are familiar with The Gorillaz, a virtual band created by musician Damon Albarn and artist Jamie Hewlett. The band consists of four digital humans – 2-D on lead vocals and keyboard, Murdoc Niccals on bass guitar, Noodle on guitar, and Russel Hobbs on the drums. They've packed stadiums of fans, collaborated with the likes of Snoop Dogg and D12, and even been awarded a coveted Grammy.

However, for every digital human that has gone onto garner fame, there are thousands that haven't taken off. How does a digital human create influence and gain a following?

First, it starts with a story. There needs to be something relatable of substance, such as a cause they fight for, an image they want to promote, or a backstory that needs to be shared.

For Ava, a digital human on the cusp of stardom, it's "her" pansexuality that makes her more relatable to her following of over 5,000. Another is Perl, who similarly promotes body positivity, often showing off the mark around her eye that discolored her skin.

Some of the stories go even deeper, creating an entire scenario around their existence, such as Lil Miquela's escape from underground sex slavery.

Creating these stories or supporting a cause is the easy part. The hard part is then finding the proper way for them to express themselves artistically because it is in their art that they begin to pull people in.

Lil Miquela's defining characteristic is her sense of style. She's very fashionable, often rocking some of the latest streetwear trends. Melissa Cohen seems to be strategically positioning her digital human brand in the food industry, often promoting Blue Apron products and posting a lot of food pictures.

Now, I know what you're thinking. What's the difference between the digital humans mentioned above, and say, Homer Simpson? He too is made of computer-graphics, has a backstory, and connects with millions of people. Is he a digital human?

Not quite. In fact, I wouldn't consider any animated characters that start on television or in movies to be digital humans because they lack one defining characteristic.

Living Life To The Fullest

The main gist of digital humans is the illusion that they are "just living life" like the rest of us. Digital humans need to share their thoughts and emotions just as much as you and I. And they do so through social media.

Even though some of them deliberately admit that they are robots, social media allows digital humans to cultivate an image of realism as though they are a regular person. Very simply, they can hit the hearts of fans without needing to be talented or entertaining in some way.

For instance, Donny Red gives people a taste of his daily fun – riding roller coasters, diving into the pool, celebrating his pet turtle's birthday. Nothing about him screams, "I'm a digital creation and I want you to spend your time and money on me." Yet, he still connects with over 100,000 fans.

Another example is Blawko, a friend of Lil Miquela, who constantly posts pictures of himself hanging out and interacting with real people. Occasionally they even do "regular people" things, such as going to a job interview.

I could even picture Blawko one day partnering with a company like Soul Machines reimagining how we interact with machines. Soul Machines recently did a concept campaign showing how McDonald's could employ interactive digital humans at ordering kiosks.

A YouTube element has been excluded from this version of the text. You can view it online here:
https://qtv1.pressbooks.com/?p=238

There's no reason that the popular, relatable digital humans like Blawko couldn't find employment through a Soul Machines provider – integrating their likeness into a corporate or service role. Not to mention, it's another stream of income for the creators of these digital humans.

These digital humans have realistic opportunities emerging because social media allows them to relate on a very basic human level and to exist as if they are living life like the rest of us.

Contrast this to Homer Simpson, Mickey Mouse, or George Jetson, who could only share their livelihood in preprogrammed, 30-minute time slots a couple times a week. Eventually, through amusement parks and merchandising, they were able to leave the confines of their Art and seemingly live a life outside of the TV. But, that came secondary.

Digital humans have the opportunity to live life on social media. In fact, this often happens before they even create an animated series, music, or art. It's a very unique position for these anthropomorphic images of reality.

And for that reason, they are becoming quite the hot commodity.

Hidden Agendas

In 2018 and moving forward, consumers are placing their trust in people over companies. Look at how swiftly Kylie Jenner's brand amassed a billion-dollar fortune. Women her age, give or take a few years, find it easy to relate to her. Meanwhile, all of her actions are deliberately crafted with the idea of making her cosmetics line flourish, her television show grow, etc...

In very much the same way, everything about a digital human can be cognizantly created – from their personality to their struggles to the way they solve those struggles – all of which are used to build trust and eventually push an agenda. In many ways, they are a marketer's ideal influencer.

Take for example, a pharmaceutical company like Pfizer who spends around $3 billion on advertising every year. One of their premier products is the antidepressant, Zoloft. Today, their route to selling this drug is through TV commercials. In just one minute, they have to build interest, garner trust, and make their pitch. A very traditional approach to advertising.

Why not instead take a small portion of this massive budget, delegate a team within their company, and build the brands of a few digital humans. If done properly, these digital humans subtly talk about their relatable issues (in this case, it would be depression). Over time, through this facade of honesty, they promote their agenda, openly talking about taking Zoloft or other medications.

I realize that this is a very sad reality – where consumers follow this fiction. But, we must realize that this level of long-term storytelling is very effective.

Look at it through the lens of a corporation. Digital human influencers are more reliable, trustworthy, and less of a hassle because all of their actions are controlled within the organization. They aren't going to pull a "Justin Bieber" and crash their Ferrari into a light pole. Or turn out to be a child molester like Jared from Subway.

Companies need spokespeople to sell their products and advertisers need to continuously reinvent their strategies to keep consumers engaged. Fictional storytelling through digital humans is an opportunity to satisfy all the parties involved. Except for the consumer, who is deliberately lied to (but what's new?).

Although the application of digital humans to Corporate Advertising is an interesting concept, more than anything, I believe that digital humans will first and foremost impact entertainment.

Six Individuals. One Digital Celebrity.

Building a digital human requires ingenuity, fine craftsmanship, and a large time investment. It's really no different than building someone's personal brand.

That's why I see teams of people executing these strategies in very much the same way that real influencers have teams working behind them. For instance, Drake has a sound engineer, stylist, writers, PR strategists, and dozens of other people all working to make his brand the showrunner. Same goes for politicians, athletes, and public speakers.

This is really not a new concept. The only difference with digital humans is that the showrunner isn't a person. It's an avatar. And what's truly unique now, is that these digital humans can be in many places at once.

Theoretically, a "digital Drake" could record a music video, shoot a campaign with Nike, and perform for thousands all at once. Most of all, he wouldn't have to worry about getting tired or worn out. He could do this day after day since there's an entire machine running behind him.

My head starts to wander to the movie industry, which is practically digitizing their entire process. Many acting moments take place in front of a green screen, all the various parts are then spliced in the scene together. And it's not just the settings that are digital.

Pioneering moments for the plight of digital human actors have already happened. Brad Pitt was almost entirely recreated using graphics in *The Curious Case of Benjamin Button*. Then there was the movie *Avatar*, where the faces of actors and actresses were morphed into entirely new beings.

There's no reason that any of the digital humans mentioned throughout this story couldn't star in one of these Hollywood blockbusters and fit right in.

In fact, it behooves the production studios themselves to grow their own digital humans and cast them in movies – thus eliminating some of the costs of hiring outside talent. The dollars clearly make cents.

But there's still one area that the digital celebrity misses the mark completely... meeting their fans.

Bringing Digital Humans To Life

Although in this digital age it's not a requirement to be physically present to build a brand. It's an aspect that's crucial to celebrity life.

The movie *S1mone* foresaw this issue perfectly. The digital celebrity, Simone, could rock the stage, hit TV, etc. but when it came time to meet the public where they were – on the red carpet, walking out of a hotel, going out to eat – she failed.

Then again, perhaps Digital Celebrities will experience physicality differently.

Augmented reality applications could potentially be used to bring these avatars to life. In very much the same way that Pokemon Go places Pokemon characters in the streets through our phone screen, we could bring digital humans to the streets as well.

Magic Leap, the maker of augmented reality glasses, recently previewed this possibility. MICA is the digital human concept they've created which essentially acts as the operating system for digital humans. Although MICA is visually completed, MICA is an alterable piece of software which brands and corporations can change to fit their narrative – and then deploy to the augmented world.

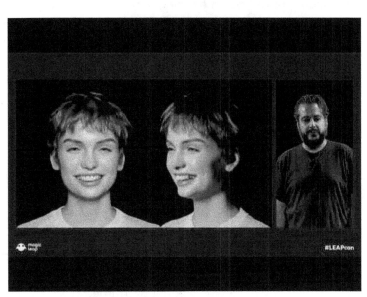

A YouTube element has been excluded from this version of the text. You can view it online here:
https://qtv1.pressbooks.com/?p=238

Perhaps a better alternative to bringing digital humans to life is in holograms. Pepper's Ghost is a 150-year-old illusion technique, where holographic images can be formed by reflecting images or videos off of Plexiglas.

Companies like Pulse Evolution, similarly use this technique today to create hyper-realistic digital humans for entertainment. Famously, they created the animated live-performance of Michael Jackson at the Billboard Music Awards in 2014. There's no reason that this technique couldn't be copied in places all around us, bringing digital humans into our field of view.

For the foreseeable future, there's always going to be some sort of "portal" required to interact with digital humans. Whether that be our phone screens, AR glasses, or holograms. That's just the nature of creating this new being.

But in a way, these digital humans are already in a different dimension. Existing right under our noses, only accessible when we take out our devices to "see" into their realm.

As more and more digital humans enter our society and we embrace them for what they stand for, there's a huge opportunity for them to rise to celebrity status and influence the way we are entertained.

What's The Verdict?

What's the verdict on Digital Celebrities? Are they good or are they bad for their respective industries, for our perspective on reality, and for our future?

Well, it's hard to say. I don't think they are good or bad... They just ARE.

On one hand, they pose a dangerous threat because they don't necessarily feel the repercussions of their actions. There's no one there to take the heat of bad behavior.

On the other hand, Jay-Z so eloquently framed it when he said, "Fame is the worst drug known to man". By creating a degree of separation between creatives and fame, well, maybe it'll turn out better for our society.

I think about the TMZ's and National Enquirer's that all make a living off dragging celebrities through the mud. Perhaps if it were a digital celebrity in these scenarios, its creators wouldn't feel quite so exposed and heartbroken.

Nonetheless, the explosion of digital humans is upon us. Graphics technology, social media, and storytellers are all merging together to bring this new "being" to life. You don't have to like them. You don't even have to pay attention to them. But, just know that they are out there. And they're the future of influence.

8. Why UBS wants a digital human version of their Chief Economist – Previewing the future of consumer interaction

At this stage in the infusion of digital humans into society, we've only come to know fictionalized digital humans.

Lil Miquela sparked the digital human phenomenon and she is a fictional fashionista created entirely in Photoshop. Then, we had a substantial follow-up from Soul Machines and FaceMe, two companies previewing how these fictional digital humans could converse with customers at kiosks in McDonald's and Vodafone.

Most use cases we've seen thus far are of fictional digital humans – fictional faces with fictional personalities, based on fictional backstories created by a team of people. However, there's a future vision in which digital humans are tethered to real people. Essentially, we're talking about the visual cloning of real people into a digital form that can be animated to interact with consumers.

Digitizing Real People

The 3D digitization of real people is nothing new. For years, with the help of Pixelgun studios, the NBA 2k video game franchise has been turning NBA players and other celebrities into realistic video game characters. This is what makes gamers feel like they're actually in the NBA and not on their couch pretending.

How can this same process be used in the corporate world?

Dead or alive, every company can point to a few employees or founders that are the lifeblood of that company – whether they are the strategic mind behind all the moves, the designer that crafts the consumer experience, or the personality that everyone associate's with the brand. These are the people that you want at the helm of every interaction with customers. Unfortunately, they can only do so much in a day.

But, what if you could bring the essence of these key player's to every single customer engagement?

This is the basis for the partnership between FaceMe and UBS (Union Bank of Switzerland), in a project known as UBS Companion.

> Decisions about wealth management portfolios require reliable, accurate insight. UBS is currently exploring the use of digital assistants to help clients and client advisors find solutions on the spot through AI-powered, frictionless access to UBS's expertise.
> UBS PRESS RELEASE

In a company as large as UBS, the people with reliable and accurate insight tend to be very busy people. Daniel Kalt, Chief Economist at UBS, is one of these people with great insight that every UBS client would like to have sat in on their meetings. This is why UBS hired FaceMe to digitize Daniel and turn him into a digital human that can interact with every customer at all times.

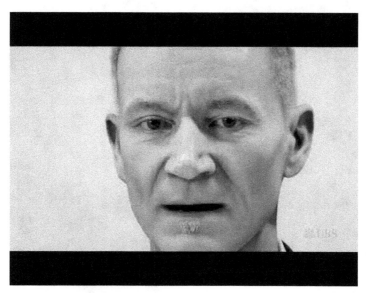

A YouTube element has been excluded from this version of the text. You can view it online here: https://qtv1.pressbooks.com/?p=240

Instead of creating a fictional character, they've turned a notable face at their company into an omnipresent conversational AI. Ideally, the digital Daniel Kalt can distill and present all the ideas that the real Daniel Kalt does, but at a much larger scale. That's powerful stuff.

Imagine if Phil Knight helped you fit into a pair of Nikes or Steve Jobs showed you how to navigate the new iOS update. This would make you feel pretty important, wouldn't it?

It's more enjoyable for consumers to interact with recognizable faces, especially if it's the face of a very important person. Digital human technology allows for these special interactions between brand and customer to happen.

Not to mention, emerging technology such as the Bellus3D app is making it easier than ever for anyone with a high-powered phone to start creating a realistic digital human. Visually, digital humans are ready to be the point of contact with customers. Just look at Desi, the digital human that'll work in McDonald's kiosks:

A YouTube element has been excluded from this version of the text. You can view it online here: https://qtv1.pressbooks.com/?p=240

The only missing piece is truly conversational AI, which can react naturally in conversations as a human would. That's the billion-dollar question that countless companies are aiming to solve. This is why talking with Alexa or Siri seems so scripted.

Until we reach this feat in AI, we'll see the early applications of digital humans (that represent real people) in roles that are largely scripted. Retail checkouts, simple banking operations, etc...

I think a really interesting use case here is political campaigning, where a large part is connecting with voters. A digital human version of a candidate adds another layer of connection, where I can ask the questions I have of candidates and get a quick response. Already, campaigners have thought through the ideal responses to every imaginable policy question. So, this would be a clean way of disseminating their views and plans to voters – instead of letting me dig through the muddied internet of political bashing.

The main point is that digital humans will play a great role in future interactions between brands and customers. Although most companies will see digital humans as a clean slate to which they can craft any fictional story. The highly effective digital humans will be clones of real people – used to maximize the trust with their fans, their customers, and their clients.

9. Why it makes sense for McDonald's (and soon others) to give machines a personality

21st-century living can be quite depressing. Most of us spend an overwhelming majority of our day interacting with phone, computer, and TV screens. It's a lifestyle, unfortunately, that probably won't change anytime soon. However, that doesn't mean we can't make it more enjoyable.

What if each one of our devices had a personality? Your phone was philosophical, always finding a way to put life into perspective. Your TV was lively, making a nine-hour Netflix binge not seem like a waste of time.

We're on the cusp of humanizing our interactions with machines – bringing more life to our days. And you should be very excited.

Operating System 2028

Touch interactions are nice and all. But let's be honest, we look like a bunch of cavemen huddled over fire whenever a screen draws our attention.

Conversational interfaces, on the other hand, are much more natural. They take our attention off of a screen. It allows us to convey the context of difficult emotions (like sarcasm), which text and touch can't even scrape the surface of. Being able to convey emotions and have more depth in the dialogue also allows the machine to capture the user's intent, which makes a huge difference.

Conversational interfaces are the next frontier in interaction. This is why we see companies, large and small, pouring massive resources into making voice work.

On one hand, you've got a company like Orbita, who's approaching voice interfaces with extreme focus – to create seamless conversational interfaces for healthcare. By focusing on a niche, they can solve for all the idiosyncrasies in that specific sphere, incorporate the necessary lingo, and truly define the standard for conversational interfaces in healthcare.

On the other hand, Google, Amazon, and Apple are all vying to create a truly conversational AI that's useful, personable, and indispensable across any and all disciplines. This multidisciplinary approach means there are endless nuances to encode and unforeseen hurdles. As a result, they have to employ linguists, comedians, and a slew of other disciplines to make machine language more well-rounded. I'm confident they'll create this conversational AI, but the path to success is much longer.

Giving a voice to machines is really only half of the outlook, though. Siri, Alexa, and other conversational AIs are all going take on a physical form through the means of Digital Humans.

The Visual Appeal

Last week I covered "Everything you need to know about Digital Humans", discussing how these new visual entities created entirely in the digital medium are poised to take over corporate advertising, pop culture, and our online personas.

We're at an interesting point in time where graphic artists have the tools to create extremely realistic-looking images from absolutely nothing.

Take, for example, the high-fashion campaign Balmain executed with entirely virtual models. To the scrolling eye, the image fits right alongside every other real (probably Photoshopped) photograph. But, the models in the campaign are about as real as imitation crab meat.

To choreograph a campaign with digital humans, you must bring together experts from various disciplines. There's a virtual clothing designer (CLO), virtual model (Shudu), the modeling agency (The Diigitals), and even a virtual photographer (CJW). Bringing all of this creative expertise and imaging software together, there's no surprise that digital humans are on the minds of every visionary.

Now, add in facial expression mapping technology such as CrazyTalk and Faceware and you've got a digital being that can express facial emotion and nonverbal cues just like a normal human.

A YouTube element has been excluded from this version of the text. You can view it online here:
https://qtv1.pressbooks.com/?p=242

Combining an intelligent, conversational AI with an animated, photorealistic digital human is a crazy combination. We're practically creating a new form of life.

Ethically, this frightens people. They fear that we'll lose control over what's real and fake online (honestly, what's new?). Before we get too deep fear mongering all the worst case scenarios, I want to dissect this outlook piece by piece.

Let's first look at how this will impact businesses.

Friendly Faces

Giving machines the ability to communicate verbally AND non-verbally essentially gives new life to the front-facing side of business.

Soul Machines is one company that imagined how McDonald's could liven up their kiosks with digital humans and conversational AI.

A YouTube element has been excluded from this version of the text. You can view it online here: https://qtv1.pressbooks.com/?p=242

How does this differ from the cashiers working the counters today?

Well for one, it's going to be a lot cheaper over time. More importantly, it allows brands like McDonald's to control their image and brand positioning across their entire company. We've all had a bad fast-food experience where the cashier was miserable and it put a damper on our day.

With these digital humans, McDonald's can curate the language and experience they want their customers to interact with, which is very appealing to all companies. In-person cashier kiosks aren't the only experiences taking on this new form of interaction.

Virtual Guidance

Ten years from now, Netflix can't rely on using the same online interface they use today. Already, people dislike scrolling through endless lists to find the right movie or show to watch.

Instead, they may employ a digital human (named Joey, perhaps), that has the personality of a moviephile – literally having an intelligent perspective on every movie and show in existence.

> You open Netflix and Joey greets you. Joey then asks you a stream of questions to help you make the ideal selection. Netflix has already collected enough data on each user to know what they'll likely enjoy. But, Joey turns this into an interpersonal journey of finding the right show, like conversing with a friend.

What's intriguing, is that all it takes is for Joey to hit the nail on the head one or two times and you're bought into this new interface. It's kind of like how early iPhones had those pointless apps that imitated bubble wrap and lightsabers, which for some odd reason intrigued people.

Over time, Joey becomes the interface through which you make all of your Netflix decisions. Heck, maybe Joey even watches and reacts during the show along with you.

Any company with a digital presence is going to feel the effects of this emerging form of voice-enabled interface. Companies will need to adopt digital human interfaces in their own unique ways. For instance, the New York Times will bring on a digital human differently from Salesforce.

A new industry will emerge that caters to providing companies with these interpersonal interfaces.

One of the early providers (on the graphics side of things) is a company called Irma Z. They are a Digital Human Talent Agency that provides companies with one-of-a-kind digital humans to fit their needs. Currently, their roster of talent is a little risque'. However, services like theirs are going to be in high demand less than ten years from now.

Overall, we're talking about an entirely new way of engaging with every single device and piece of software we use today. It's a massive change that won't come easy. But, with these steps, we begin entering a realm of ultra-personalization and experiences of our own choosing, known as Imagined Reality.

10. How Domino's is leading us into the era of conversational interfaces

Have you ever wondered why an overwhelming number of conversational AIs are voiced by females? It seems as though in the process of humanizing the machines around us, we may be taking a step backward in gender bias. Alexandra Whittington, Futurist at Fast Future, elaborates on this problem:

> The issue here is that we may be seeing the replication of gender stereotypes and unconscious biases in the design of these systems, which could have massively damaging consequences for society if the process continues unchecked.
>
> **ALEXANDRA WHITTINGTON**, *A VERY HUMAN FUTURE*

Alexandra goes on to compare the conversational AIs in assistant roles (predominantly female) with the conversational AIs in productive roles (predominantly male). For example, we have Siri who's upholding kind of the receptionist role of yesteryear versus Ross who's an AI paralegal sifting through thousands of cases on a daily basis.

Perhaps it's an attempt to cover up the Big Brother invasiveness with a trustworthy "Big Mother" voice. Maybe it's that the pool of AI developers is too homogenous (white and male). I really don't know.

However, less than a decade in, we've barely even scratched the surface of conversational AIs and virtual companionship. I hear Alexandra's (and many other people's) concerns. But, I have reason to believe we're entering an era in technological design where this won't actually be a concern of ours.

Conversational Design

We've spent the last twenty or thirty years at the mercy of developers designing the way we interact with technology. We're only now beginning to understand how large tech companies psychologically-engineered their products to create a sort of dopamine dependence on them (cough, cough... Facebook).

In contrast, we're beginning to see conversational interfaces that are focused on making enjoyable (not addictive) experiences. DialogFlow is one company in particular that empowers companies to create unique dialogue interactions with their customers. Dominos, for instance, worked with DialogFlow to create the flow for customers to order pizza with Siri, Alexa, and Google Assistant. After ordering a pizza through it, I can honestly say I felt more comfortable ordering with their voice assistant, as opposed to their website, where I always feel like I'm being upsold a lava cake or something.

The name of the game is no longer addictive design. It's humanistic design. It's about creating an interpersonal connection with technology – where the technology helps you be a better, more well-rounded "you".

We're ready for a more symbiotic relationship with technology – an essence I think Apple captures with their Apple Watch campaign: "There's a better you in you". The Apple Watch is an ever-present, intelligent machine that interacts with us and pushes us to be better people. Fairly soon, this will be a feature of conversational AIs.

By now, there's plenty of data out in the metaverse about each one of us. All of this data which can be used to actually get to know us (not just our shopping preferences). In other words, conversational AI companions (like Siri and Alexa) will be able to build meaningful friendships with us.

By design, conversational AIs are great listeners, which actually sets them up to be caring friends in the future. Additionally, they are all-knowing helpers. This is how we know them today. Siri can answer all the questions Google Search can answer.

One minute, they'll teach me the ins and outs of Photoshop and the next minute they'll ask me what's stressing me out? It's an interesting duality that we'll quickly grow attached to.

There's an obvious parallel we can draw to really understand this concept of a virtual companion.

Virtual Companionship

Do you remember Clippy from the Microsoft Office suite back in the day? Essentially, it was a cute paperclip figure that would hang out in Word documents and solve any questions you had about the software.

Take Clippy and add in the ability to work with you across all software and devices. It can help with any questions you have and even takes the time to get to know you on a personal level. Wouldn't you say that's a powerful virtual companion to have?

Perhaps what's most important, as I alluded to earlier in this article, is the ability to customize their visual appearance and personality.

We're already seeing this customization of conversational AIs occurring with Siri Shortcuts – a little-known feature of Apple products where you can curate Siri's actions. I'm expecting that Apple (and their competitors) will build out this functionality to offer vast customization. Pretty soon, Siri's personality traits will be controlled by toggle switches we can move around and basically create the ideal virtual companion for our tastes.

I asked Ryan about this:

> Presence is very important to me. I'd like my virtual companion to be chillin on my screens all the time. Visually, I'd like them to be goofy looking, so that I smile whenever I see him. Perhaps an old man from one of *The Far Side* comics. Also, I'd like him to have an edge. Someone I can banter with and get some witty criticism here and there. I'm definitely not interested in a kiss-ass servant. That doesn't appeal to me at all.
>
> **RYAN**, SENIOR PRODUCER AT INEVITABLE/HUMAN

All of this is becoming increasingly possible with data and advances in conversational AI.

Overall, there's a lot of exciting fringe technology out there to be enthralled by – VR, AR, Quantum Computing, Artificial General Intelligence, the list goes on. However, the innovation we should really be interested in actually involves the relationships we build with our technology.

I see virtual companions playing a crucial role in making our relationship with technology more enjoyable and more symbiotic.

11. This 2090 prediction teaches us about climate change's impact on the future of work

The Prediction:

ANNUAL ECONOMIC DAMAGES FROM CLIMATE CHANGE COULD ADD UP TO NEARLY $700 BILLION BY 2090,IF NATIONS FAIL TO MAKE MEANINGFUL CHANGES TO ADDRESS THE DANGERS.

– MIT TECHNOLOGY REVIEW

You don't have to look far for a climate change article aimed at your heart – deterioration of beautiful coastland, destroying the magnificent coral reefs, the extinction of innocent aquatic and insect species – but when's the last time climate change was directed at your wallet?

A report by the National Climate Association (brought to my attention by the MIT Technology Review) told a completely different story about climate change that hadn't really occurred to me. Their predictive data told a climate change story of decreased productivity, economic repercussions, and mortality.

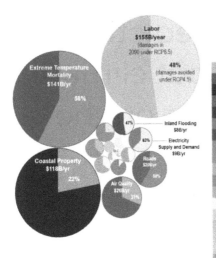

Annual Economic Damages in 2090		
Sector	Annual damages under RCP8.5	Damages avoided under RCP4.5
Labor	$155B	48%
Extreme Temperature Mortality◊	$141B	58%
Coastal Property◊	$118B	22%
Air Quality	$26B	31%
Roads◊	$20B	59%
Electricity Supply and Demand	$9B	63%
Inland Flooding	$8B	47%
Urban Drainage	$6B	26%
Rail◊	$6B	36%
Water Quality	$5B	35%
Coral Reefs	$4B	12%
West Nile Virus	$3B	47%
Freshwater Fish	$3B	44%
Winter Recreation	$2B	107%
Bridges	$1B	48%
Munic. and Industrial Water Supply	$316M	33%
Harmful Algal Blooms	$199M	45%
Alaska Infrastructure◊	$174M	53%
Shellfish*	$23M	57%
Agriculture*	$12M	11%
Aeroallergens*	$1M	57%
Wildfire	–$106M	–134%

This report really came as a shock to me. Yes, the timeline is a little ambitious. I mean, it's like a pre-World War I Henry Ford predicting what would happen in the auto industry seventy-five years later in 1990. It's inconceivable. However, what I do like about this report, is that it uncovers some perspectives that we rarely discuss when it comes to climate change.

The report talks about the economic losses due to heat exhaustion. The report speaks to the increased heat-related deaths. It covers the effects on simple infrastructure, such as roadways. These are three of the top five estimated economic consequences of climate change, yet, it's the first time I've heard them in climate change narratives.

I've come to realize that our environment may "feel the heat" of climate change, but it hadn't occurred to me that the very lifestyles we live and the way we work would be affected as well.

> Scientists have long recognized that extreme temperatures can reduce productivity, as well as lowering lifetime earnings, widening wealth disparities, inciting violence, and increasing suicides and deaths (see "Death will be one of the highest economic costs of climate change").
>
> Faced with sizzling temperatures, workers compensate by

changing the timing, location, level, or type of work they do, all of which can affect their output and pay.

The effect is particularly pronounced with manual outdoor labor like farming and construction, but it shows up even in air-conditioned factories or offices, Walker says. In the United States, auto plant production drops by 8% during weeks with six or more days above 90 °F, according to a 2012 study.

JAMES TEMPLE, MIT TECHNOLOGY REVIEW

You tell ConAgra foods that extreme heat will kill their crops and they'll engineer a crop that needs less water. You tell ConAgra foods that extreme heat will make their workers less productive and they'll think about their bottom line – and either want to make a positive environmental impact or pour resources into robots and drones that can withstand the inhumane conditions.

A Lesson in Futurology

More than anything, this is a lesson in futurology and how futuristic challenges are rarely single-faceted. There's always more than meets the eye if you're willing to look further than the obvious. In the realm of climate change, there are unforeseen consequences (and thus opportunities) that don't get discussed.

For instance, companies that sell equipment for outdoor activities – Schwinn bikes, Goalrilla basketball hoops, football cleats – will all feel the effects if people are spending less time outside. Is there a way to adapt these outdoor products?

Hotter average temperatures will undoubtedly increase the wear on roofing shingles. Is there an opportunity to create a more efficient tile?

Regardless of whether humans do in fact contribute to climate change (I'm not here to discuss that), there's a chance that just a couple decades from now we'll be living in more environmentally strenuous times. These pain points scream for innovative opportunities.

12. Tasty, edible crickets may solve the impending food crisis

The planet must produce more food in the next four decades than all farmers in history have harvested over the past 8,000 years. With the global population set to reach 10 billion by 2050, many scientists have come to the consensus that we're going to enter a desperate world food shortage very soon if we don't make some changes.

I'll be honest, for an American under the age of 80 (like me), it's hard to imagine the concept of food rationing. Any time of day, I can walk three blocks in any direction and feed myself until I'm gorged. And for the past half-century, the developed world has really only known a food surplus. But this fact could be quickly shifting.

> Climate change, urbanization, and soil degradation is shrinking the availability of arable land, according to the World Economic Forum. Add water shortages, pollution, and worsening inequality into the mix and the implications are stark.
>
> **JOSEPH HINCKS,** TIME

This means that scientists and farmers alike are tasked with finding creative solutions. Innovative farming hubs, such as the Food Valley at the Netherland's Wageningen University & Research, show how farms of the future will use indoor vertical farming techniques to make farming more efficient.

We're aware that most food production is inefficient. Another way of looking at the problem, though, is that the inefficient farming is dependent on what we choose to eat. For instance, the animal farming necessary to satisfy our taste for meat takes a massive toll on our resources.

> **A kilogram of beef is about 30-times more demanding on the environment than a kilogram of plant protein. For a sustainable future, I suspect that quite radical change to our diets is needed.**
> **JOSEPH HINCKS,** TIME

The obvious solution is to scale back our consumption of meat and the need for animal farming would decline. This means consuming our protein from a different source.

One of the most compelling alternatives is Soylent which manufactures meal supplements that cover all of one's dietary needs – turning optimal nutrition into three shakes a day. It's a fascinating community of die-hard fans that I'd even compare to the early Apple craze.

An emerging (and far less palatable) diet is eating insects as a main source of protein. No, seriously. It's a theory that's not all that off-base.

> **Two billion people in the world eat insects as a part of their normal diet, approximately the number that owned a smartphone last year.**
>
> **DEREK THOMPSON,** THE ATLANTIC

Tiny Farms is one company that is making a big bet on crickets to be used as a reliable source of protein. Right now, they largely produce the crickets for use in pet food, but there's no reason spice-fried crickets can't take off with humans.

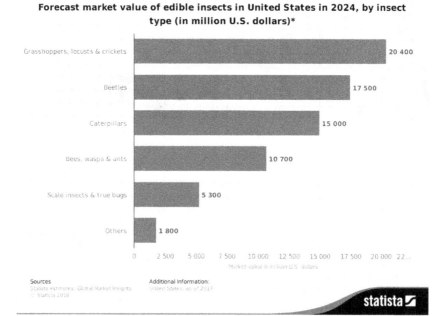

Forecast market value of edible insects in United States in 2024, by insect type (in million U.S. dollars)*

Edible insects isn't a popular concept in the US today. Currently, the **estimated market value of edible insects amounts to $406M USD and is forecasted to increase to about $1.2B USD by 2023**. All we need is a Gatorade-like product for edible insects to arise and this forecast above will be vastly surpassed.

It's evident that we cannot go on producing and eating food the way we do. The solutions are present, but will only take place when we are ready to change as a culture.

I have faith that the growing "food conscious" movement will spark this change. It could be any of the Netflix documentaries detailing the ugly side of factory farms. It could be a TED talk that reverberates across the globe.

One generation can create a massive cultural change. And dammit if I have to eat a cricket to save the planet, then pass the Sriracha because I'm going in.

13. How self-driving cars will make cities healthier (in a way you'd never expect)

The year is 2030. Your Mercedes-Benz S-class is having transmission troubles, so you take it into the dealership. Half an hour passes and a manager approaches you with the news:

> Welp, the repair is going to run you about $3,500. Your transmission is about to poop out on ya. We can have you back on the road in a couple of days, or... you can trade in your car and switch over to our Unlimited Autonomous Network. We remove all the hassle of owning a car. Any time of day, you can hail one of our network cars and within two minutes you'll be on your way to your destination. You'll never have to worry about car maintenance or insurance again. We take car of it all. And it's only going to cost you $250 per month. What do you say?

It's an offer you can't refuse. And perhaps a future we cannot avoid.

Car manufacturers and ride-sharing services are all buying into this concept of on-demand networks of self-driving vehicles that take people to their destinations with style and ease. It's a business model that replaces consumer car ownership with ride-hailing subscriptions.

There are a few reasons why the automotive industry is taking this so seriously:

- AAA estimates the average cost of owning a car at $706 per month.
- Cars spend 95% of their lifetime in the parked position.
- Self-driving car technology is making significant advances year after year.

Services that can significantly undercut the cost of owning a car (without sacrificing the convenience) will likely see success. By replacing individual car ownership with fleets of cars constantly moving people from Point A to Point B, never needing to sit idle in a parking lot somewhere, inadvertently you remove a lot of cars from the roadways.

> The number of passenger vehicles on American roads will drop from 247 million to 44 million, opening up vast tracts of land for other, more productive uses.
> **TONY SEBA,** RETHINKX

City-dwellers are likely to be the first demographic to ditch their car for an autonomous ride-hailing subscription and the side-effects are going to be major.

> There won't be any parking lots or parking spaces on roads or in buildings. Garages will be repurposed – maybe as mini loading docks for people and deliveries. Aesthetics of homes and commercial buildings will change as parking lots and spaces go away. There will be a multi-year boom in landscaping and basement and garage conversions as these spaces become available.
> GEOFF NESNOW, 73 MIND-BLOWING IMPLICATIONS OF A DRIVERLESS FUTURE

Browsing the streets of most cities, you'll find that parking lots and garages are about as plentiful as Starbucks. In Los Angeles, there are nearly 2.5 million parking spaces that can be repurposed. Across the nation, there's an estimated 40,000 parking lots and garages – all of which might one day be obsolete.

This is space that can be repurposed in many ways. Here's one:

Parking Lot Farms

Cities have horrendous access to fresh produce. To create a regular salad – lettuce, tomatoes, carrots, cucumbers, and radishes – we're talking about a collective travel time in the thousands of miles. This means that one salad, I ate for one meal, on one day of the week probably traveled more than I have in the past decade. That's horrible in terms of nutrient freshness and carbon footprint.

This is why innovative urban farming initiatives are emerging.

In the heart of NYC, inside a 40-foot shipping container, Square Roots is creating the Future of Urban Farming. Utilizing a mixture of LED lighting, vertical farming, and hydroponics techniques, Square Roots is growing fresh produce in a gravel parking lot. And with lots of success.

A YouTube element has been excluded from this version of the text. You can view it online here: https://qtv1.pressbooks.com/?p=250

No joke, shipping container farms like Local Roots can yield between 2-6 tons of leaf lettuce per shipping container per week while using a fraction of the water to do so. It's an extremely efficient method that allows fresh produce to be grown anywhere at any time of the year.

Imagine filling a parking lot with these. You're talking about an entire farm in half a city block. Now that's innovation.

The best part is that local restaurants and customers have to walk just a few blocks to get fresh produce, lengthening the product's lifespan and disintegrating its carbon footprint.

> I can't wait for the day when I can walk to my local parking lot to pick fresh strawberries.

This is a market I see exploding in the next five years with the help of CropBoxand Modular Farms – which are manufacturing ready-to-use shipping container farms.

There are of course downsides to this high-growth vertical farming. The amount of energy required for lighting and climate control is fairly large. Thus, to turn a profit they are limited to growing expensive produce such as leafy greens, strawberries, and tomatoes. However, we're less than a decade into this new form of farming and I'm excited to see how they'll continue making this type of farming more compelling.

Vertical farming isn't the only way we can repurpose parking lots, garages, and spaces. However, bringing fresh produce closer to cities seems way better than building another towering apartment complex.

By 2030, we'll begin seeing repurposing of public garages for other uses, along with services (such as shipping-container farms) that make these transitions simple.

14. AI paints a portrait. Christie's sells it for $435,000. What's the world coming to?

When science and the humanities collide, it's usually a battle of existential proportions. However, this time the disparate communities came together to make a major statement (and a few dollars).

Last week, the high-brow auction house Christie's sold a painting called *Portrait of Edmond Belamy* for an astounding $435,000. The portrait isn't visually appealing. The person isn't recognizable. And it really doesn't fit into any historical period. So how did it fetch such a price point?

Well, it was created by a machine learning algorithm. That's right. Its creator was an AI network!

The team behind the algorithm, an artist collective called Obvious, trained the AI network on thousands of portraits from the 14th to 20th centuries – teaching it how to replicate and refine portraits of its own (you can read about the process here and their help from the open-source community). The result looks unfinished and unsettling. But, I'll let you decide if it's your style or not:

Now, I want to make this perfectly clear that this does not mean computers can be creative. In fact, the marketing of this painting was a little misleading. AI-generated art is far from an autonomous process. There's still a heavy amount of human intervention required.

You can draw a parallel between AI-generated art and art class for 10-year-olds – where an art teacher walks them through each step and occasionally intervenes to make sure it's not a total disaster.

Regardless, this is still a momentous event. More than anything, it's a sign of acceptance – that perhaps the art community is ready to explore the artistic medium of artificial intelligence. It's very possible that the anonymous buyer, who paid 45 times the estimated price point, likely saw this as a "Bitcoin moment" and could signal a surge in algorithmic art auctioning.

Skilled   algorithmic   artists   like Robbie   Barrat and Mario

Klingemann will be ready to cash in on this movement. Although, is algorithmic art truly art?

Art Without Intention

A few months ago I got into a Twitter debate with a very respected technologist, Benedict Evans. His argument (and the argument of many other doubters) is:

> Ryan thanks for sharing I agree with the author of the paper that we're in an era of where AI enables artists to make art. However, when I look at projects like @lilmiquela give it 20+ years and I think the algorithms will be able to generate art and contribute socially.
> — QuHarrison Terry ? (@quharrison) September 25, 2018

If we're defining a machine's intent against how humans have intent (through consciousness), then Ben is correct. AI will not create art until we achieve Artificial General Intelligence (AI that can think for itself).

Isn't it possible, though, that we should define intent differently for machines? Perhaps machines have intention through specific prompts and lines of code. In this case, then AI is highly capable of creating true art (and already has).

Another way of thinking about this argument around intent is the way we consume artwork.

There are of course critics and consumers that are just as interested in understanding what Picasso was mentally experiencing while painting *The Old Guitarist* as they are interested in the painting itself. This is Ben's argument of "intent" being crucial to art.

On the other hand, there's the notion that we must separate the "art" from the "artist" before consuming a piece of art. Otherwise, we'll analyze the artist instead of the artwork. In other words, "Who cares who the artist is? This work moves me and inspires my thoughts." In this case, intent doesn't matter.

These two schools of thought will likely argue the definition of AI-created art for a long time to come. Yet, I do believe they will agree about one major thing…

A Revolution in AI Assistance

We're entering an era where artists of all kinds will be extremely empowered by artificial intelligence tools. The ideation, refinement, and distribution phases will all have significant AI applications to help artists produce more quality work and reach the audiences that desire their style.

Artists are constantly asked, "Where do you get your ideas from?" It's a tough question to answer because the ideation process is generally intangible. However, researchers are finding ways for computers to augment the early creation phases of 3D objects. This is one instance of an algorithmic artist creating a prompt for a human artist to later fill in. I can imagine an AI-plugin for Photoshop that analyzes an artist's style and can inspire that artist by prompting them with the first few random lines or textures of a new piece of art. Sometimes the first lines are the hardest part – a part of the creative process that AI may be able to solve.

Refining and editing one's artwork is an equally important part of the creative process. In the music industry, we've already seen huge progress from companies like LANDR which provide musicians with an AI that'll master their raw tracks. In visual art, Color-Correct is one early example of machine learning that helps clean up photographs. We'll likely see many more applications that assist artists with their editing process.

And of course, when it comes to distribution, social media is one instance of AI helping artists reach their fans. However, we'll likely see improvement upon the AI in distribution to help artists identify potential markets and opportunities.

All artistic disciplines are in for large-scale interference from AI tools in the next decade. Savvy artists that embrace this change will find themselves pushing the boundaries of human creation.

15. AI in Marketing: Generative Adversarial Networks (GANs)

Every company, no matter the size or industry, must have a sense of urgency in finding ways to bring AI into their organization.

> While some companies – most large banks, Ford and GM, Pfizer, and virtually all tech firms – are aggressively adopting artificial intelligence, many are not. Instead they are waiting for the technology to mature and for expertise in AI to become more widely available. They are planning to be "fast followers" – a strategy that has worked with most information technologies. We think this is a bad idea.
> Mahidhar & Davenport, HBR

It's safe to say there isn't a single org out there that is doubting the prevalence and propensity of artificial intelligence to disrupt their industry. There's really no objection.

However, the idea that you can wait for the easy tool or enterprise integration of AI is very risky. Because there won't be simple, umbrella solutions of a sales AI, marketing AI, human resources AI, etc... That's just not how AI will progress.

> In most cases AI supports individual tasks and not entire business processes
> Mahidhar & Davenport, HBR

In 2018, it's very important that you think of automation as if you were a sniper in the military – with one target (task) in mind. Do not think about how AI can improve your entire marketing department. Think, instead, how AI could be used to generate content ideas, which is one task among the entire marketing strategy.

It's this focused, task-level thinking that has inspired more than 2,700 AI projects at Alphabet.

Look for tasks within your organization that are repeatable and gather lots of feedback/data. These are the low hanging fruit.

Before you begin that process, though, it's important to learn the capabilities of AI to inform where it can be applied on a task-level. I think there's no better place to start than GANs.

Fans of GANs

Generative Adversarial Networks (GANs) are a class of artificial intelligence that operates by pitting two neural networks against one another (hence, adversarial).

> One neural network, called the generator, generates new data instances, while the other, the discriminator, evaluates them for authenticity; i.e. the discriminator decides whether each instance of data it reviews belongs to the actual training dataset or not.
>
> You can think of a GAN as the combination of a counterfeiter and a cop in a game of cat and mouse, where the counterfeiter is learning to pass false notes, and the cop is learning to detect them. Both are dynamic; i.e. the cop is in training, too (maybe the central bank is flagging bills that slipped through), and each side comes to learn the other's methods in a constant escalation.
>
> Skymind AI

It's a system that is optimal for producing, evaluating, and reworking a creation, which is why it has been referred to as the creative-side of artificial intelligence.

Most notably, Robbie Barrat created a GAN for the purposes of artistic creation. His code was used by a team called Obvious, which trained the GAN on 18th-century portraits and eventually sold one of their digital creations at a Christie's auction for $435,000.

> GANs' potential is huge, because they can learn to mimic any distribution of data. That is, GANs can be taught to create worlds eerily similar to our own in any domain: images, music, speech,

prose. They are robot artists in a sense, and their output is impressive – poignant even.

Skymind AI

Today, GANs are being tested in various creative endeavors. This Redditor is experimenting with GANs to push sneaker designing to new areas we've never thought to explore. Robbie Barrat, the same man behind the aforementioned artistic GAN, has since moved on to high fashion – using GANs to create entirely new clothing color palettes and augment the role of creative director at a fashion house.

I'm very intrigued by the application of GANs to the arts, however, the marketer in me is more interested in using GANs to assist us in marketing tasks.

GANs in Marketing

Recently, two researchers at Stanford ran a GAN experiment on automating the creation of Airbnb listing descriptions. Any marketer worth their weight in gold knows that the way you describe a product is equally, if not more, important than the product itself. The theory was that the way in which a listing was phrased would directly correlate to its occupancy rate. Armed with data from 40,000 Airbnb listings they taught a GAN to optimize descriptions.

In the end, they came to the realization that aside from keyword packing, the listing descriptions didn't affect the occupancy rate quite as much as other characteristics: location, amenities, and home type. What's important is that they had a theory, acquired needed data, and ran a test. I'd expect that more experiments with better data will follow suit and push this theory forward – ultimately with the goal of optimizing descriptions for products, services, and other digital products.

Taking things in a different direction, the Pose Guided Person Generation Networkis a GAN research project aimed at manipulating a subject within an image into different poses. The value in this would be that product photographers (hopefully by 2038) could focus on taking one great picture and allow the GAN to recreate all the other product angles. This would translate to monumental time and cost savings for an e-commerce business – given that the average cost of shooting one product is upwards of $30. You can see the early progress of this below:

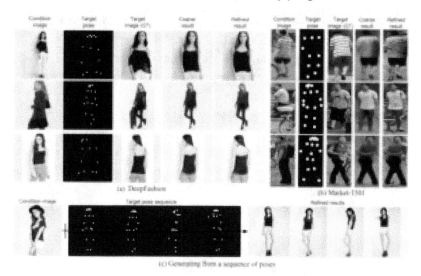

While both of these GAN research projects have obvious benefits to any e-commerce business. I feel that the outlook is even greater. The true value is in teaching a GAN that produce any sort of convincing text or image, just by giving it a set of parameters.

One of the practitioners at the forefront this is Janelle Shane of the blog AI Weirdness. Her text generating GANs have produced quirky things such as Dungeons & Dragons character bios and ear-grabbing CNN headlines. If you have a free minute or two, I'd highly suggest you get lost on her website for a little while. You're going to learn a lot about neural networks (such as GANs), in a very entertaining, peculiar way.

I realize that the GAN projects I've outlined above are not nearly as convincing as putting in the human elbow grease and doing it yourself. However, this is an area of AI that once it clicks, the output will outpace the work of hundreds, even thousands of workers. Not to mention, we're looking at GAN just a few years in. After all, the theory behind GAN is just four years old.

What to Takeaway?

Right now, you should optimize for learning the current experiments happening with AI and posing questions of AI's capabilities. Ruminate on the different ways AI may fit within your org, talk to knowledgeable people about what these tests may require, and think about what type of data you should be collecting.

Proprietary data will be the differentiating factor between companies that successfully implement AI and those that fall behind.

What data are you collecting today that is unique to your organization? If the answer is "none", how might you start collecting proprietary data sets?

16. AI in Marketing: Intelligent Shopping Assistants & Personal AI Replicas

The value that comes with shopping at a high-class store like Bergdorf Goodman's in the heart of NYC's Fifth Avenue, is not the fancy clothes. You can get fancy clothes in a number of places. The true value is getting paired with a personal shopper that first develops a bond with you and then fits you in a style that feels a part of you.

Today, this is a completely foreign shopping experience at 99% of stores. But it'll soon be commonplace in many of the physical stores that survive this retail apocalypse. It won't be humans providing this experience though. Instead, we're seeing a glimpse of the technology pushing these experiences forward, from the company TwentyBN and their intelligent shopping assistant called Millie:

A YouTube element has been excluded from this version of the text. You can view it online here: https://qtv1.pressbooks.com/?p=256

The value of an intelligent shopping assistant like Millie is that it never forgets a purchase, a preference, or a previous visit. It's how retail stores will bring all of their valuable shopping data from the virtual world into the physical shopping experience.

When deployed in a store that a consumer frequently visits, this intelligent shopping assistant will ensure routine purchases flow uninterrupted into your shopping cart while simultaneously predicting/pushing you toward other items you might enjoy (think about shopping on Amazon.com but in a physical store). It's basically automated consumerism.

With the right verbiage, Millie can then prompt follow-up purchases, "Well you can't get a new pair of shades without a fresh outfit to go along with it." And then it proceeds to pair it with a red belt and red suede shoes.

The problem is that a business cannot solely optimize data usage for selling more goods, especially if it's at the expense of the customer's feeling of free will. Everybody hates buyer's remorse and if it occurs because an AI pushed you into a purchase, well that just looks bad on the company.

By 2031, we'll see the first intelligent shopping assistants enter retail stores for the purpose of improving the consumer experience.

The short-minded companies will exploit intelligent shopping assistants to make a lot of money. But they won't last. The companies that flourish long-term will use this new data portal (intelligent shopping assistants) to create better customer relationships, as Bergdorf Goodman's does.

AIs Develop Customer Relationships

AI assistants clearly have a long way to go here, considering there is really no personal connection developed between Siri and me – despite Siri being in my life for the past five years. However, it doesn't mean that a virtual assistant is not capable of developing real connections with us. In fact, there is perhaps a no better example of this type of virtual assistant than Replika, the AI chatbot that mimics your unique personality.

> Replika is designed to listen and empathize, like a good friend. For the first time, we are experiencing an AI that understands people's emotions and plays to our personalities.
> Quick Theories
> Your Replika is designed to remember everything you tell it, learning about you, your moods, tastes and preferences, and then to use that information in future conversations.
> Xenia Grubstein, Narratively

When I communicated with Replika, it asked me questions that some of my closest friends have never asked me. And for whatever reason, I felt comfortable responding with true feelings.

With over two million users, Replika is a chatbot that isn't interested in exploiting consumer behavior. Instead, it's interested in creating relationships beyond the data. It develops trust and can converse with people for hours.

Apple, Amazon, Google – they want their conversational AIs to create close relationships with their users. However, the main barrier is trust. It's hard for people to answer personal questions to Alexa or Siri because there are behemoth corporations behind them. Replika, on the other hand, represents "the little guy" and doesn't appear to have any ulterior motives.

Truthfully, it's only a matter of time before Apple, Amazon, and Google find ways to build relationships between their virtual assistants and users, as Replika has already proven.

Imagine the power of Alexa (with all that Amazon customer data) combined with a Replika-type conversational personality. Essentially, they will have created the personal shopper/point-of-contact for every single consumer, which can be deployed across online and physical stores.

More than Commerce

From styling suggestions to shopping preferences to personality traits, they'll not only know the data of our decisions, but also the deeper feelings behind our habits. That's a deadly combination.

At this point, it basically becomes our initial point of contact with other friends and businesses. In the article, Google Duplex brings an exciting update to the earliest piece of modern technology, I describe this possibility of an AI like Google Duplex which may one day speak on our behalf.

Being the holiday season, we can all relate with the pressure to find great gifts for people. Well, what if your AI shopping assistant would also speak with friends and family about what gifts you might enjoy. That way, nobody has to go through the pain of giving or receiving a gift that is absolutely not a good a fit.

Additionally, what if before you got on a sales call or before you met with a new client, you could inquire their personal assistant on all those surface-level "discovery questions" we all know and hate. Then, when you did meet up with them, you already had the foundational knowledge needed to build a relationship and best serve their needs.

Given the large amount of data exhaust (as Michael Dempsey puts it) we create from emailing, messaging, online shopping, web searching, etc. these aren't that absurd of realities.

The Takeaway

There are two ways you can get involved in this future change. One, you can create a chatbot. Two, you can lean into and create an experience on an existing conversational platform. I'll explain each in detail below.

Chatbots are a low-risk way of dipping your toes into scaling customer relationships. What's good about chatbots is that there are many tools and tutorials to help you create this seamless dialogue with customers. And when done properly, they connect and convert customers extremely well.

Of the thousands of chatbots out there, one of the more effective deployments I've come across is VIPKid. It's a Beijing-based education technology company aimed at China's tens of millions of students. The company connects Chinese pupils with fluent English-speaking tutors in the United States and Canada. They have been using a rule-based chatbot since the summer of 2017. It has qualified and helped onboard more than 9,000 teacher partner leads, improving the experience for candidates and saving the company 1,000+ hours of human time.

On the other hand, if you have a solid brand presence already and sufficient resources, you might try building an experience on existing conversational platforms, such as Google Home or Amazon Echo.

> Right now, web and mobile is a mess; each time users have to buy something or use a service, they have to download an app and create an account. That's where voice-based systems can really evolve. Voice User Interface's stop users from needing to install different apps or create separate accounts for each service they use. Instead, it brings them all together through conversation. Why download an app for booking a flight or ordering a taxi when you could just ask one chat interface to do it?
>
> Nick Babich, Shopify

There aren't a ton of great case studies in this realm to look at yet. But, Uber is probably the front-runner – ordering food with Amazon Echo. In due time, we're going to see a lot of services get it right on these platforms.

I could see Yummly, a visual and semantic recipe search engine and aggregator with over 20 million users building out a (branded) Voice User interface that walks you through every step of the cooking experience on a device like the Amazon Echo Show. This would mitigate the step of loading an app every time you're in the kitchen and create an even more seamless cooking experience for their users.

At the end of the day, Voice User Interfaces will be much harder to get right and require a lot more time and resource investment. But those that get it right will create a more natural, convenient way of interacting with their customers, while also bringing personality to their brand. Not to mention, verbal communication is extremely accessible to people of all ages and demographics.

17. AI will pick (and make) the songs you love in just 6 years

Music has a rich history of technological and digital augmentation. Think about Peter Frampton and Jimi Hendrix using "talk boxes" to make their guitars talk for them. Or how about the billions of people influenced by the computerized sounds of pop music from Michael Jackson, Prince, and Madonna. This is partly why the music industry is already accepting a revolution in artificial intelligence.

Music is an industry where the technologically unsavvy musicians can't necessarily keep up. A musician without access to studios, equipment, and high-tech software may be able to rock a small live audience. But they cannot produce and master their sound to national syndication quality.

Compare this to other art disciplines. Visual artists can use oil and canvas and still be pictured in the Museum of Modern Art. Writers can type on 1950s typewriters and still influence the entire country with their prose. The equipment makes no difference.

> This technological barrier to entry in music precipitates into a massive opportunity for artificial intelligence. It's why we're seeing the adoption of AI in the music business unparalleled by any other art form.

Take, for example, LANDR, which is an AI audio mastering tool that's disrupting recording studios. Essentially, LANDR takes on the crucial role of sound engineer, helping artists master their sonics. With millions of analyzed sounds in its archive, LANDR can also help artists find the sound unique to their identity. Best of all, it's accessible (all online) and affordable (just a few dollars).

Sound engineering isn't the only role AI entering either. It's also behind the instruments.

Amper is an artificial intelligence composer, performer, and producer that empowers artists to instantly create and customize original music for their content. As far as I know, they've got a major hit under their belt with an artist named Taryn Southern. And many more to come.

Similarly, AIVA is an AI composer making major progress in music production, however, with a different approach. Instead of catering to artists, they want to be the personalized musician for everybody (particularly gamers at first). They recognize that there are many moments and emotions in life that lack music. AIVA fills this by making great quality compositions personalized to the listener.

We're going to see more programs like Amper and AIVA emerge that'll give pop artists a catchy loop, rap artists a hard beat, and every listener a song just for them.

When Kanye West introduced the Hip-Hop world to Auto-Tune on his album *808s & Heartbreak*, the world was appalled by the technology. Later, T-Pain would bite the style and create an entire career around the tool. And now nearly every hip-hop or pop artist uses the tool in some capacity on a regular basis. AI music production tools are very much in the same boat.

Will any of these AI tools single-handedly create the next *Thriller*? Not on their own. But, it lowers the barrier to entry and puts the possibility to create magic in the hands of more artists. For this reason, AI tools are going to drastically elevate the quality and variety of music that makes it to the mainstream.

By 2026, 55% of the Top 40 Billboard singles will be partially written or produced using AI tools.

> Today, Spotify sees about 20,000 new uploaded songs a day. This equates to over 7 million songs a year. And that's just one streaming platform. There's also YouTube, SoundCloud, Apple Music, etc.

This number of music creation will only amplify over the next years with this widespread access to professional production tools.

How can we, as consumers, expect to weave through all of this material to make sure we still discover the great music? How can record labels expect to weave through all these artists and make sure they're offering opportunities to the right ones?

The Bad Side of Data

Take any historic record label and you'll find at the heart of their success is a great A&R (artists & repertoire) Executive. They are the lifeblood of a label. They are responsible for spotting emerging talent and identifying where the industry is headed. In a way, they are futurists of the music industry.

When an A&R is on top of their game, like L.A. Reid when he signed the 14-year-old Usher or John Hammond when he discovered the 18-year-old Aretha Franklin, they influence entire genres of music.

When an A&R is off their game, like RSO Records passing up on U2 or the numerous labels that didn't care for Jay Z, they might be responsible for their label's demise.

Because their job deals with recognizing new sounds and not just riding the quick trends, A&Rs always tended to have a great ear for music and the cultural zeitgeist. Then, about fifteen years ago, with the advent of digital music platforms, record labels replaced their musically-inclined A&Rs with data-minded businessmen. The folks in charge of supplying the record labels with fresh talent began thinking far more about metrics than actual sonic influence. It became a game of marketability – where image and branding outweighed talent.

This is largely where the industry is today. Labels give their biggest budgets and opportunities (radio spins, marketing, etc) to artists whose images they can control and get clear data on. I don't believe this is for a greater cultural conspiracy. Rather, they want to make sure they make money. Therefore, taking risks isn't how it's done.

It's all about to change, though, with the emergence of the AI-powered A&R.

The Good Side of Data

Because music has gone digital and streaming platforms collect so much data, the opportunity for intelligent systems to analyze this data with greater, thoughtful scrutiny is here.

The AI-powered A&R is an intelligent system that analyzes music streaming data, fan engagement on social media, and other data to discover the next big talents in music along with gaining strategic insight into the artists they've already signed.

Some of the more popular AI-powered A&Rs are Asaii and Instrumental. There's also Sodatone which was bought by Warner Music Group.

How does the use of AI-powered A&Rs differ from the last couple of decades of data dependence?

The difference here is that they're taking into account more streams of data and the models for analysis are beginning to reach their true potential. This shifts the data discussion to emphasize quality over quantity.

> For instance, let's say they're analyzing two new artists: Alphonse and Bambino. Alphonse has 500 fans but consistently engages each for an average of 35 minutes a day (10 songs). Bambino has 6,000 fans but on average engages them for only 12 minutes a day (3 songs).
>
> Even though Bambino gets more than five times the stream time as Alphonse, in theory, an AI-powered A&R would choose Alphonse over Bambino.
>
> This is because the data shows far more fan engagement for Alphonse, who's defined his audience persona. He knows the people that love his music and now it's all about finding the others just like them. Bambino, although with a bigger audience, is a little more discombobulated as far as finding his ideal audience.

Ideally, just a few years from now, an AI-powered A&R is to be able to find the next hit song when there are only 65 listeners. Contrary to the A&R today who might not discover the song until it's at 1 million hits.

I know it's a cliche' to say that the AI will help humans, not replace them. However, this is truly the case for an AI-powered A&R.

If we refer back to the number of new music generated every year (7 million songs on Spotify alone), it's clear that finding quality talent depends on breaking through the noise. This is where the AI-powered A&R will excel – analyzing thousands of new songs and artists a day to narrow the field of emerging talent. This should give record labels the chance of bringing back some of the human A&Rs that have a great ear for music and what the next sounds to influence the culture will be.

Who knows, with AI composers like Amper entering the field of music, one of these AI-powered A&Rs might one day sign an AI composer to their record label. Wouldn't that be ironic?

18. How AI-enabled toys are molding our children [PART 1]

The other day when I was walking through Target I witnessed the most shocking interaction between a mother and her toddler. Well, actually it was a lack of interaction. One of them was acting like the other didn't even exist, completely immersed in their smartphone... and it wasn't the mother.

Here was a four- or five-year-old, working a smartphone as if it were their left arm. It was truly a match that made sense. Kids are enthralled by stimulation. Anything fast-moving, visually mesmerizing, or just plain different is going to capture their attention. The smartphone is the perfect stimulator.

Initially, this image made me sick to my stomach. Was this really the way that millions of people were raising their kids?

However, I quickly realized this reality is here to stay. Personally, I don't see my device usage fading anytime soon, which means that the kiddos are going to continue copying us. Now, we can be hypocritical and tell children "do as I say, not as I do". But honestly, I don't really see that having good results.

Instead of playing the hypocrite, maybe it's time we get behind the technology movement and actually use it to create better learning environments for our kids.

We're already witnessing many legacy toy brands use advanced technology to animate their once inanimate toys. Pokemon's augmented reality app is just one great example of a stagnant brand reinvigorating itself with new technology. Another brand I'm particularly impressed with is Hot Wheels.

Hot Wheels created what they call an Intelligent Race System. Essentially, kids can race a remote control car around a 16-foot track against a robot racer. It's a physical track with a robot opponent. That's pretty cool, in and of itself. However, just like a computer opponent has different difficulties, so too does the Hot Wheels robot opponent. As the kid gets better and better at playing the game, the robot's difficulty also increases. Hot Wheels says it learns to better itself through AI, but I'm a little skeptical. I think it just has different settings.

Nonetheless, this indicates a particular wave we're about to see in toys. And that is an AI-enabled toy that learns and grows alongside its user.

Learning with the Youth

Not long ago, researchers at SoftBank Robotics stumbled upon a groundbreaking realization that a robot toy is more valuable to a child's education, not as a teacher but as a student. In other words, by creating an intelligent robot that purposely makes mistakes – thus prompting the child to correct them – you actually do much more for the child's education than lecturing them. Some refer to SoftBank's education robot, NAO, as a dunce robot. But, it's actually a concept based on educational truths.

Teachers have long understood that knowledge can be further encoded in a student's brain when they have to explain what they've learned to another student. It's called peer learning.

This is vastly different from what we normally expect of interactions with intelligent machines. Generally, we expect Siri or Alexa to yield results. We ask them a question and demand an answer.

SoftBank Robotics, on the other hand, proposes that we design AI Educational Toys to always display slightly less intelligence than their child user. As the child "teaches" the robot what they're learning, the robot steps up its game to continuously challenge the child.

Similarly, Joseph Michaelis, a doctoral student at UW-Madison, has designed a learning companion with some of his colleagues. Their robot, Minnie, accompanies a child while they read aloud, responding with thoughtful comments. If the child reads a frightening scene, Minnie might respond with, "Oh, wow I'm scared."

"Learning companion" is a fascinating vertical for AI-enabled Toys and robots. By occupying this educational space and growing with the user, they achieve toy longevity.

Toy Longevity

We all know how quickly children grow tired of toys. My cousin keeps a bucket (and I mean a BUCKET) of discarded toys that their three kids have lost interest in.

However, imagine if books like *Green Eggs & Ham* rewrote themselves over time to continuously intrigue and better your child's vocabulary and comprehension. What if Monopoly, after you played it for a certain amount of time, evolved into a deeper, more realistic game about investing and building finances.

It's hard for us to wrap our minds around a physical product evolving before our eyes (like we do as humans). But this is exactly what AI Toys are designed to do – evolve and develop alongside a child.

Do you really want a toy to grow with your child?

Yes. Actually, you should. Not only could it be cheaper on your wallet, but it's an optimal tool for learning because it can tailor its message to the level of skill a child exhibits.

Contrary to most toys on the market which are stagnant with a singular function, AI Toys are multi-functional, incorporate intelligence, and change over time.

One of the greatest assets or features of an AI Toy is its longevity. It has the staying power to outlast other toys that come and go with the seasons.

Interestingly, "learning companion" is just one narrow role that AI Toys are occupying in kids' lives...

19. How AI-enabled toys are molding our children [PART 2]

In China, where families are limited to bearing one child, AI Toys play the role of friendly Robot Companion as much as they do educational aid. It may sound absurd that a robot could ever be a friend, however, this unexpected vertical for AI Toys is really taking off:

> ...an estimated 30 million AI educational robots were sold in China this year, and next year the number is expected to exceed 100 million
>
> SERENITIE **WANG,** CNN

BeanQ is one of these Robot Companions. It's a social robot equipped with similar voice intelligence that we see in Siri, Alexa, and Google Assistant. More than anything, toddlers use BeanQ as a "question-answerer" since we all know how young-ins love to pepper people with questions. Additionally, the small, kidney-shaped robot displays emojis and emotional intelligence to make interactions more lifelike. And it's pretty cute to boot.

A similar product here in the US is Jibo. Jibo imagines their device as a great social companion for kids – in a way documenting their early life, engaging the kid when their parent(s) isn't around.

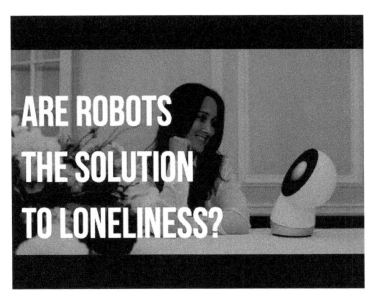

A YouTube element has been excluded from this version of the text. You can view it online here: https://qtv1.pressbooks.com/?p=263

Techie families may invariably dive into buying these AI Toys because they are intriguing. But, lots of families are turned off by the privacy concerns and the fact that they're teaching their kids to talk to a machine. However, Ryan had an interesting take on these social robots:

> As the second child in my family, by the time I hit about 12 or 13, my parents felt comfortable leaving me home alone if they were going out. I loved being treated like an adult, but also felt lonely in our cold, dark basement watching TV late at night. A product like Jibo intrigues me because I can imagine how an animate robot would've made me feel safer. Just seeing Jibo make "shoulder shrugs" and movements here and there would've made me feel like a friend was close by.

Ryan alludes to a strong conceptual argument in favor of these Robot

Companions: they aren't here to replace interactions with friends and family, but rather to fill in the gaps when those people aren't present.

Parents get busy and friends aren't always free to hang. Robot Companions, on the other hand, are always an open-ear. In this way, they are the futuristic version of a pet animal. They are a physical presence used for comfort and emotional connection.

A Friendly Robotic Presence

Just five years from now, in 2023, the global market for consumer robots is expected to reach $14.9B, increasing from $5.4B today. Bloomberg adds that in the US, the market will exceed $4B by 2025.

This is why Amazon is working on creating a robotic version of their Echo voice-activated speakers. It's why Alphabet bought (but has since sold) Boston Dynamics and reportedly have other robot projects under wraps today. The companies with the biggest balance sheets are getting in on this industry, which is a sign of great potential.

Most notably, Apple has co-signed a brand of Robot Companions known as Anki. Anki's latest companion is called Vector – a tiny, tractor-shaped robot with a lot of personality. Vector is spatially aware which allows it to roll around the house without getting into any trouble. It basically just kind of chills and acts as a friendly robotic presence.

Some may look at Vector as a useless piece of plastic. But, Anki is priming a futuristic market of robot companions that roam our houses. Although Vector can't even make us a piece of toast today, many iterations down the line, it will.

We're only a few years into this market of AI-enabled Toys and Robot Companions. Anki, Jibo, BeanQ, and SoftBank Robotics are all laying the cultural groundwork for this market to flourish in the future. They're getting people comfortable with the idea of a robotic presence in their household.

Imagine a company introducing an all-in-one robotic housekeeper like Rosie the Robot today. They may as well be selling us a UFO because the masses just aren't ready for this.

I believe this is why most companies are focusing on making cute toys that intrigue little kids. Children have tremendous buying power, largely fueling the madness of Holiday shopping. And by tailoring their products to kids, they are seeding the market for long-term household robotics users.

Today, AI Toys and Robot Companions are serving the early education market. In eight years, they will have mastered the art of conversation with people of all ages. And by 2038, 90% of American households will be able to afford a household robot.

There's a plethora of functions that robots will fill in our future lives – from educational aids to friendly companions to chore do-ers. I want to make this message loud and clear that the home is a sacred place, a place we can create however we'd like – high-tech, low-tech, no-tech. It's very important to realize that robots can serve a great purpose in the home, but the choice is yours as to what level they'll be present.

20. AI doesn't have a sense of humor. But it does help comedians create material.

Every week on Quick Theories, we look at how an industry is changing to predict how we might fit in with this change. However, there's an equally important question, a question that Buffett and Bezos both live by:

What's not going to change in the next ten years?

This is why we're going to look at an industry that won't be derailed and "revolutionized" by artificial intelligence – an industry where its players have the choice to use AI, and even then, the algorithms won't likely give those people an advantage. That is the humor industry; more specifically cartooning.

At the peak of his distribution, Gary Larson's *The Far Side* comic was syndicated to over 1,900 newspapers and read by millions of people every day. For fifteen years, he changed the way people look at life. That's the power of cartoons and comic strips.

Not much has changed technologically for cartoonists since Larson's heyday in the early 90s or even Charles Schultz's inaugural *Peanuts* cartoon in the 50s. The only difference now, is that some of the savvier cartoonists have turned to Reddit and webcomic apps, instead of newspapers, to gather their audiences and make a living.

The Oatmeal, Mr. Lovenstein, and *xkcd* are three famous webcomics of our day that may one day be compared to the scale and impact of *Calvin and Hobbes, Dilbert,* and *Garfield.*

At its essence, there's no inherent need for new technology in the cartooning industry. The lack of advanced software has not caused it to fade from existence. The simplicity doesn't make it less funny in our digital world. In fact, it is perhaps the simplicity of cartoons that people gravitate toward. For the foreseeable future, it's an unchanging industry.

But, that's not to say that AI cannot be advantageous to cartoonists.

Bot-created Comedy

Can machines be humorous? It's an odd question, but it's the thesis behind Botnik Studios – a community of writers, artists, and developers using machines to create things, some funny, some not:

> The collective began when Google DeepMind wanted to make a bot for The New Yorker's caption contest, which the magazine's cartoon editor from 1997 to 2017, Bob Mankoff, created. Noticing an uptick in similar projects trying to "solve" creative tasks with automation, Mankoff and Brew created Botnik, which sought to augment instead of automate.
>
> "We use machines to enable new kinds of human creativity. Botnik Studios... grew from the user testers for our first web app, a predictive text keyboard called Voicebox that offers word suggestions based on any source text you feed it."
>
> **GEORGINA USTIK,** THE NEXT WEB

They've trained about a dozen predictive text keyboards on scripts from the *X-Files* and *Seinfeld,* beauty ads, and even pancake recipes. It's not fully autonomous. The process is really augmentative, where the machine suggests about a dozen words at a time and the user gets to choose from the suggested words to string together sentences (the words change after each selection).

Using these keyboards, the collective has created a spoof installment in the Harry Potter series titled *Harry Potter and the Portrait that Looked Like A Huge Pile of Ash*. Also, in 2019 they're releasing an album called *The Songularity* which was created using a keyboard trained on Scottish folk ballads and Amazon product reviews.

Honestly, their results are nonsensical. But when performed live, I actually got quite a kick out of it. Therefore, the AI cannot be funny on its own without a little help from a human.

Upon digging a little further, I found a comedian that's actually brought AI onto the stage with him. Piotr Mirowski, a former Google Engineer, has developed a robot with conversational AI which interacts with him during his act. The two get on stage and go about having a conversation.

> What A.I. is good at, Mr. Mirowski said, is saying unusual things that challenge the human improviser to work harder, which can increase satisfaction when they manage to make a scene work. "Improv is like intellectual and mental tightrope walking," he said. "The robot is kind of making the tightrope longer."
>
> **ALEX MARSHALL,** THE NEW YORK TIMES

Piotr's words resonate with the same challenges as Botnik Studios. The biggest deterrent to a comedic AI is that they don't understand dialogue and cannot read and relate to an audience. The good thing is that every major tech company is pooling massive resources into achieving an AI that can casually converse for hours. At which point, I think will see robot comedians.

For the time being, AI will have to play the role of comedic inspirer.

AI-augmented Cartooning

I tried out Botnik's Sigmund Freud-inspired predictive text writer and created these two lines:

- Dream content may readily separate the patient from their brain.
- Medical geographers are actually made during sorrow.

The incoherence (edging on slight profundity) made me chuckle. Just for fun, I sent the two lines conjured up using Botnik's predictive writer over to a webcartoonist I know, just to see his response. This is what he sent back:

"Frank, buddy, don't you want to be remembered as the Lewis and Clark of the Large Intestine?"

This was actually quite fun. I mean, never in a million moments would I have thought about the concept of a "medical geographer". I wouldn't say this is my best work, but I can see how the process would help me explore the nooks and crannies of wordplay we never imagine. I think I'll probably do more of this in the future and hopefully be able to get more work out the door.

PENN WRIGHT

In theory, we could probably witness the first AI-generated comic strip in just a few years. With the billions of memes on the Internet, which have already been rated for their "funniness" based on the number of likes. It wouldn't be that difficult for an engineer to create an AI that can come up with its own captions for new memes. However, this is just not a lucrative problem to solve, so there aren't many people at it.

For the time being, as is the case with Botnik Studios, Piotr Mirowski, and Penn Wright, AI will help humorous people continue to find new ideas.

What's the Point?

You're probably wondering why we'd even want AI that can be funny. Well, the way I see it is with an AI-sidekick or AI as competition, comedic figures can be empowered to bring more comedy into the world. Humor is absolutely the best medicine out there. Unlike other art forms, where scarcity increases the value. The more comedy the better. Jerry Seinfeld elaborates on this:

> My entire adult life is just making comedy stuff. For some reason, it's important to me to make as much of it as I can. I imagine a woodchuck has a similar mindset: 'I've got to chuck wood, as much as I can, because that's my thing.'
> **JERRY SEINFELD, COMEDIANS IN CARS GETTING COFFEE**

Comedy has the luxury of an honest feedback loop. Laughter is an involuntary response. If people laugh, it means that the joke was funny. If people didn't laugh, then it's not funny. With comedy, the good stuff sticks. And sometimes you have to go through a lot of unfunny material to hit a solid joke.

To be frank, I'm not sure I have the answers when it comes to AI in comedy. What are your thoughts on this unexpected application of artificial intelligence?

21. Google Duplex brings an exciting update to the earliest piece of modern technology

One hundred and forty-two years after Alexander Graham Bell made the first phone call, we're on the brink of an unbelievable advancement in telephone automation.

> In May [of 2018], Google made quite the splash when it unveiled Duplex, its eerily human-like voice assistant capable of making restaurant reservations and salon appointments. It seemed to mark a new milestone in speech generation and natural-language understanding, and it pulled back the curtain on what the future of human-AI interaction might look like.
>   Karen Hao, MIT Technology Review

Google Duplex was so different and exciting because it achieved a form of conversational AI we hadn't heard yet. It talked naturally, spontaneously, and empathetically. You could even go so far as to say that it passed the Turing Test, basically meaning that its communication was indistinguishable from that of a human.

A YouTube element has been excluded from this version of the text. You can view it online here: https://qtv1.pressbooks.com/?p=267

Six months have passed since that magical day with very little updates. Google Duplex is still only available on the newest Google Pixel phones. However, an international competitor just launched with some similar news. Alibaba – which is basically the Amazon + Google of China – announced a conversational AI just like Duplex that can handle simple service calls with the nuance of human conversation.

In the midst of a conversation about rescheduling a package delivery, Alibaba's conversational AI eloquently handled an interruption, a nonlinear request, and even implicit intent. This is leagues ahead of the virtual assistants we interact with today.

Why must we be paying attention to these technological updates?

Automating Calls

Every major tech company is firing on all cylinders with voice assistants. It's only a matter of time before Apple launches a Siri update where it can inquire about the availability of a book at your local Barnes & Noble. Fairly soon, there will be an Alexa skill to make calls for dinner reservations.

It's not that Google, Apple, Amazon, Alibaba, and Microsoft are seeing into the future and finding that we're going to be using our voices more. No, they've all just set their minds to crafting this automated voice calling behavior in the future. To ignore that this'll happen is to ignore a collective $3.5 trillion of corporate market cap that are buying into this future.

The progression of Duplex and similar conversational AIs will go as follows:

1. Simple customer service tasks
2. Complex customer service tasks
3. Business to business communication

Simple customer service tasks – We're already seeing this live in action with Duplex and Alibaba. This is where the conversational AI can make calls on a consumer's behalf and inquire about simple tasks. For instance, making dinner reservations, scheduling a package delivery, asking about product availability, etc... Conversational AIs will master these simple customer service tasks within the next three years.

Complex customer service tasks – Think about the last time you needed to troubleshoot a problem or dispute a billing issue with your telecom/internet provider. A robot probably asked you a series of questions, put you into a specific category, and then connected you with a representative. I'd venture to guess the entire process took over 30 minutes.

About four years from now, Duplex (and competitors) will be able to call customer service centers on your behalf and dispute/troubleshoot problems. (Ironically, this means that two conversational AIs will be talking to one another). We, as consumers, waste a lot of time engaging with the current customer service call centers, therefore, the value of a conversational AI talking on our behalf would be huge. Especially if it can get results.

This leads me to the final area Duplex (and competitors) will enter.

Business to business communication – Although it's a very complex undertaking, there will come a time when Duplex and other conversational AIs will be used by businesses (not just consumers) to reach out to leads, set-up meetings, and close deals. The savvy businessmen will train Duplex to give their company's "elevator pitch", thus acting as a front-of-house salesman – bringing in potential clients nonstop.

We're at least seven years away from Duplex gaining these full conversational capabilities, but it doesn't mean that smaller business initiatives cannot be executed in the meantime. The people that begin thinking about this today will have swift implementation when it does come around.

The Takeaway

Duplex and Alibaba have given us a taste of conversational AIs that are natural, spontaneous, and empathetic. It's what we've been dreaming of ever since Apple launched Siri in 2011, Amazon's Alexa in 2015, and Google Assistant in 2016. This is the progress that should excite people of the possibilities once again.

The main takeaway here is that over the past decade we've been coerced away from our telephones as tools of commerce. Today, any efforts in the telephone space are half-baked and stale.

The shiny object of the Internet has led us astray from this extremely valuable and personable way of connecting and doing business. However, there are many signs pointing in the direction of vocal communication as a means of doing great business in the next decade. Those who find novel ways of reintroducing voice communication into commercial practice will be seen as great marketers and visionaries.

If you want to get involved, the first step is assessing how you use the telephone and other vocal communication in your business today. When's the last time you called up your company's customer support center to give them feedback?

The next step is really thinking of unique ways your business might consider using the telephone as a marketing platform and ultimately how these conversational AIs will fit in one day. Have you ever used public conference calls as a way to bring in new leads?

Concretely, if you're very excited, go out and purchase yourself a Google Pixel phone and learn the territory. I think there's also something to be said about creating Alexa skills unique to your business. It's not Duplex-level, however, Amazon is pouring lots of money into making Alexa a well-rounded communicator.

We've all forgotten about the telephone as a platform for marketing, sales, and customer service. Any use of the telephone in business has become predictable and expected. This means the opportunity is ripe to reconsider the use case of the telephone and surprise customers with novel experiences.

22. Today, Siri can read to you. Soon, Siri will read for you.

Finding time to read these days is tough. Between social media algorithms constantly flooding us with notifications and our tendency to choose more entertaining alternatives, it's not uncommon to go long stretches without reading something meaningful, fulfilling, or impactful. Not for a lack of desire, though.

We all want to be able to read that growing stack of books. We all want to feel informed of what's going on in the world. Personally, I find myself wanting to achieve Warren Buffett's benchmark:

> **"Read 500 pages...every day. That's how knowledge works. It builds up, like compound interest. All of you can do it, but I guarantee not many of you will do it."**
> **WARREN BUFFETT**

Clearly, in these days of exponential information, finding time to read is a billion-dollar problem. This is why Blinkist and other manual summarization tools exist. But, machine-learning experts believe that the answer lies in AI.

Using machine-learning to summarize and make sense of text isn't an easy problem to solve and actually has been a part of scientific theories for quite some time. However, it's just in the past couple of years that promising improvements have been made.

A little-known tool known as SMMRY is using AI to summarize articles in a matter of seconds. It analyzes the prominence of words, determines the weight (importance) of a given sentence, and compresses each article down to the most important 7 sentences.

Ironically, I stumbled upon a fairly scientific paper discussing this topic and used the SMMRY tool to extract the insights for me. It eliminated some of the necessary background information to fully comprehend the article, which you can expect when it kills 77% of the text. Yet, I still got the main gist and feel smarter after using it.

On the other hand, Salesforce is attacking the problem a little differently. They are teaching an algorithm from examples of good summaries, an approach called supervised learning. They also emphasize an artificial attention to the text to help ensure that it doesn't produce too many repetitive strands of text (a common problem with summarization algorithms).

Both of these tools have a long way to go before we can trust them to summarize at the level of, or higher than, the human brain.

Nonetheless, you really can run rampant with all the possible use cases of a highly effective AI Summarizer. It would do wonders for graduate students researching for their Senior Thesis. Paralegals could find the precedent they are looking for in a fraction of the time. And everyone would feel empowered to pour over books and books of information.

Ideally, a well-functioning AI Summarizer would be integrated within our existing device interfaces.

By 2028 Siri will have integrated this summarization functionality – whereby I scroll through my timeline, stop on an article, and prompt Siri: "Hey Siri, what's this article about?" – receiving a thoughtful, effective summary of the document before diving deep into it.

What's stopping you from reading every day?

23. Virtual facelifts and AI-generated makeup. When will the absurdity end?

Video chatting is a pillar of communication these days. In WhatsApp alone, users made over 340 million minutes of video calls per day. This doesn't take into account the dozens of other video chat apps like FaceTime, Google Duo, or Facebook Messenger.

And even if you're not making video calls for pleasure, there's a great chance you're using Google Hangouts, Skype, or Zoom to hold virtual meetings at work.

With all these video chats taking place, the opportunity to improve the experience is paramount to beating out the competition.

Apple's Animoji and Snapchat filters show us that there's a way to spice up video conversations. I can hop in FaceTime, have a conversation with Ryan as a unicorn. If Ryan wants to be a lizard, that's his prerogative.

In a way, video chat alterations are becoming an entire economy. It's only natural that we're going to continue making our appearances unnatural, very much in the same way that our digital photographs have lost their ties to actual reality. Honestly, is there a single photograph on Facebook, Instagram, or the entire Internet that hasn't been hit with a touchup tool like Photoshop or the filters in every camera app?

Virtual Facelift

For years, I've been using Zoom to hold digital meetings with clients and coworkers. Only just the other day did I come across a very intriguing option in their menu called "Touch Up My Appearance".

With the click of a button, Zoom covers up blemishes and baggy eyes, smooths wrinkles, and makes my skin glow. It's a virtual facelift compliments of Zoom. In just a couple of years, the virtual facelift will come baked into every video chatting platform, whether you realize it or not.

If it's any indication of this wave, it's happening to the iPhone XS in a scenario people are calling BeautyGate. Essentially, the camera in the XS has a few algorithms that automatically touch up people's appearances to remove blemishes, shadows, and smooth the skin's appearance with selfies. Some people love the way they look in these pictures, while others think it appears unrealistic.

Nonetheless, the virtual facelift is just the start of this wild economy. What comes after the virtual facelift?

AI-generated Makeup

A year ago, Sephora showed us the first version of AI-generated makeup. They were a little ahead of their time with their Virtual Artist app. Users can virtually apply different shades of lipstick and other makeup to their digital image. It's a way of trying on makeup without going into the store.

What's AI-generated about that experience?

Well, the logical next step is to apply the technology to video chat applications. If Zoom can touch up my appearance real-time, then what's stopping them from applying lipstick to my lips in real-time?

Pretty soon, users will be able to open the Sephora profile builder, choose their lip color, cheek contour, eyeshadow, etc... and apply it to their digital image. When they open FaceTime, their virtual makeup choices will be overlayed on the video. This is what one of my female coworkers had to say about this idea.

> It's odd that I can do all my work from home. What's even odder is that I do my makeup and get dressed up to not leave the house for work, just because I have a few virtual meetings every day on Google Hangouts. If Google Hangouts offered virtual makeup, then I'd just use them to apply my makeup. It would save me hours every week.

All it takes is for Kylie Jenner or Rihanna to hop on this wave and it'll become wildly popular. This is how beauty products companies will "future-proof" their companies and solidify their places in digital economies.

Honestly, this won't be just a women thing, either.

Digital Beautification for Men

Similarly, men will be able to erase the wrinkles and blemishes, but also choose the way they appear on a deeper level.

Different jawlines come across differently on a subliminal level – some appear strong while others more vulnerable. Depending on what the situation calls for, men will be able to touch up their appearances to appear a certain way in the eyes of the person they're chatting with. It'll be subtle shading and contour techniques that accomplish this.

Naturally, there's already an app called Manly that adds six-pack abs and beards to photos. Of course, these will soon be features of the real-time video appearance alterations as well.

The facial recognition and facial mapping technology already exist to make these real-time video alterations a feature of every video chat application.

This makes me question: what will the App Store for FaceTime appearances look like?

By 2024, video chat applications will offer a variety of AI-generated makeup, virtual facelifts, facial reconstruction, and other digital appearance altering tools.

This will be a popular way for people to control the appearance they present through video chat applications. We're going to see an entire economic boom around real-time video alterations. Look at all the hoopla that FakeApp is causing with fake video creations.

Pretty or Pretty Ugly

The one thing that must remain a part of this technology is the user choice. If the technology is applied to our faces in video applications whether we choose or not, there are going to be some major issues.

As I mentioned before, we're already seeing this algorithmic overlay with the BeautyGate iPhone camera issue. This is a problem because there is no universal idea of beauty. What one person sees as pretty, to another person is pretty ugly. This is why there must remain an element of user customization.

Nonetheless, we're about to enter a really odd time.

> We are going to become so accustomed to AI generated "makeup", "smart" email responses, and software-defined personalities that within five years, being "authentic" will be seen as a highly valued job skill or a circus oddity.
> CHRIS DANCY

Soon, it'll be natural for our digital appearances to be unnatural. I'm not particularly thrilled for the psychological effects this is going to bring to society.

24. Would you attend a wedding in virtual reality?

It's crazy to think that one of the most anticipated events of the year was a wedding. Just a few weeks ago, over 29 million US citizens tuned in to watch the Royal Wedding. And while many major TV networks capitalized on the broadcast of this event, they missed one huge opportunity in virtual reality.

Broadcasting Live in VR

This year marked a big year for VR broadcasts. NextVR brought us the entire NBA season in virtual reality (including the Finals). Fox Sports is bringing us 64 World Cup matches in VR.

So, why didn't they broadcast the Royal Wedding in virtual reality?

While Drop would've allowed people to follow along with the Royal Wedding as if they were in a newsroom setting. I'm thinking even above and beyond this.

The way I witnessed some of my friends and family geek out over this event weeks in advance, I know for a fact some of them would've coughed up money for a premium VR experience (especially if it meant sitting next to David Beckham). They might've even bought a headset just for this one occasion.

Last year, this wouldn't have been a compelling argument to make. But, as I've stated before:

> After spending a considerable amount of time in the VR space back in 2014-2016 and not seeing much happen since then, Facebook's launch of their second VR headset, the Oculus Go, is something to finally get me amped about VR again.

Recently I attended a live VR concert with Ben Slater, Co-Founder of RightMinder, who was on the other side of the globe. We were both absolutely blown away by the experience:

Hey @reuben_thedark watching you LIVE in VR thanks to @nextvr and @oculus! People are just absolutely FREAKING out how damn good it is! Your harmonies are amazing...digging it. You are an AMAZING band...thanks so much. PS Watching from Australia. pic.twitter.com/DxK0dkbcMi

— BEN SLATER ? (@iambenslater) June 12, 2018

Attending this concert in my virtual form, made me think about the relationship between technology, communication, and our connectedness to one another. And really how all new communication channels undergo the Cyber Contact Progression.

Attending this concert in my virtual form, made me think about the relationship between technology, communication, and our connectedness to one another. And really how all new communication channels undergo the Cyber Contact Progression.

Cyber Contact Progression

The way we communicate with each other in cyberspace must constantly evolve to satisfy our need to feel connected and welcomed by others. Change is an inevitable part of communication channels (Email, SMS, Facebook, etc...) and can be defined by three progressive stages: **Extreme Ambiguity**, **Concentrated Efficiency**, and **Momentary Liberation**.

Extreme Ambiguity (Stage 1) is the first defining characteristic of any new communication channel. No one knows the best practices yet and there aren't enough people using it to make it a convenient means of communication. Over time, though, user adoption increases, new capabilities are presented, and they then enter the stage of...

Concentrated Efficiency (Stage 2). At this point, users understand the best practices for the channel. Communication is very efficient between current users and a mass of net-new users arrive. However, if you've ever made juice from concentrate before, then you know that when you add a little too much concentration to the mix, the drink goes sour. This is when the channel becomes overcrowded with people, oversaturated with corporate advertisements (to compensate for the rising costs associated with user growth) and ineffective for communication. Leaving a gap for...

Momentary Liberation (Stage 3). This is when a close derivative of the previous channel (either an updated version or new channel altogether) is introduced that solves this inefficiency problem. It's a moment of liberation because the noise seems to disappear. But, beware, because this feeling of liberation is only momentary. There's surely a new channel itching to take its place.

Let's Look at a Few Examples

Email was an extremely ambiguous service to start. No one really knew when they should send an email or a fax. Some early email systems even required the author and the recipient to both be online at the same time. Eventually, the kinks unfolded and it became one of the most efficient ways of communicating professionally and personally. Unfortunately, email was so effortless that it became oversaturated with spam and advertisements to the point where the only liberation was declaring email bankruptcy (leaving that email altogether).

Another example is Facebook. I remember a time when my friends and I didn't know whether to use it as a tool to stalk our crushes or share funny videos on our walls. Facebook then launched the Newsfeed, the purpose of Facebook became clear, and it emerges as the most efficient channel for staying up to date on your friends' lives. Currently, though, we are in need of liberation because Facebook has become an advertising haven to the point where you barely see friends' content. The momentary liberation could come in the form of an update to their algorithms or a new platform altogether (Oculus Go VR headset?).

Take any digital communication channel that allows us to chat with one another and you'll find that it goes through the Cyber Contact Progression.

Currently, virtual reality is in this Extreme Ambiguity stage. No one really understands the purpose and there's a lot of experimenting going on. But, Oculus Go is on the verge of breaking into the Concentrated Efficiency stage.

Going back to the concert I attended with Ben Slater. We both recognized how easy it was for us to communicate with the other virtual concert attendees – truly serving its purpose as a means of efficient communication.

This made me ponder how other experiences in Oculus Go will help transition this tool from the Extreme Ambiguity stage to the Concentrated Efficiency stage. And in the spirit of the Royal Wedding, I decided to look into a VR wedding.

A Better Wedding in VR

When thinking about experiences that'll be impressive in virtual reality, weddings are interesting partly because there's a massive monetary incentive to be the first mover in that industry. Already, the wedding industry is worth $72 billion annually in the US alone – supporting an entire economy of caterers, ceremony and reception venues, florists, photographers, hair stylists, limo drivers, bands, DJs, and even wedding painters.

Every couple that takes this huge step in their life must balance their dreams with their budget... the budget usually taking a big hit. But, virtual reality weddings have a chance at cutting this cost down to a fraction (if you want to go virtual).

In VR, couples can book St. Peter's Basilica for the ceremony and transport all their guests to beaches in the South of France for the reception, without having to fly people all over the world. InsiteVR is already well on their way to providing users with the architecture necessary to build these realms.

Additionally, florists could take their time creating one magnificent centerpiece that puts the Royal Gardens to shame. Then, uploading their arrangements digitally and duplicating it for every table.

When it comes time for the night's entertainment, onto the stage come Maroon 5, Elton John, U2, and any other superstar artists (they've chosen) to give live performances in VR.

And with the clink of their VR headsets Shawn and Dawn's marriage was sealed

Not to mention, attending one of these weddings would be practically frictionless. Guests wouldn't have to worry about finding / buying something nice to wear, clearing their schedule, or traveling to the location. Instead, a few moments before the ceremony starts, they place on their Oculus Go, choose an outfit for their avatar, and take their seat. Think about how great this would be for friends and relatives that are either immobile or live far away.

And let's not forget about the food.

Catering a VR wedding – 300 people in 300 different places – at first sounds like a logistical nightmare. But, the infrastructure already exists with food delivery platforms like Postmates, GrubHub, and UberEATS. Every guest could order a dish from a local restaurant that they enjoy – instead of just being given an option between steak, chicken, or vegetarian. And it may even come in at a lower cost to the bride and groom, who often spend between $30-100 per plate.

All of this and more is easily accessible in virtual reality. The social experience wouldn't quite be the same, but you'd still be able to interact and engage in conversation with the people you want to see. Also, you wouldn't have to worry about your uncle getting way too drunk and causing a scene.

When can we expect this?

Realistically, we're 8 years away from seeing a VR wedding that could rival the experience of a traditional wedding. But, the people that will bring you impressive VR weddings will start creating them this year.

Who's going to be the first florist to work with graphic designers to bring their creations into the virtual realm? Which DJs and bands will foresee this opportunity, branding and enhancing the VR wedding entertainment? Which food delivery service will create a portal for wedding guests to easily order and coordinate their reception food?

Of course, there are many wedding traditions that will be upheld. But, I see VR weddings as an opportunity to reinvent or add to the traditions we've come to expect. an experience unique to that communication channel.

This may make you uncomfortable to think with. Although, when has a comfort zone ever allowed anyone to grow?

Getting out of your comfort zone

Comfort is nice. And we should all find comfortable places to relax.

However, comfort is stagnancy. It's our body's signal that no growth is taking place. Think about it: beds are the most comfortable in the morning when the day is calling. But, if we stay in comfort, we cannot get out and seize the day. This is a parable for all of life's situations.

The person who only exercises comfortably may never achieve their physical goals. The salesman who only fills their day with comfortable leads will never land the big fish that gets them the promotion.

All day we have opportunities to do things at a comfortable, sustainable pace – to minimize stress on ourselves. But it is in uncomfortable situations which lead to leaps in our growth.

25. Walmart changes the world again – this time with virtual reality

High-risk, life-threatening jobs have been using virtual reality (in a way) for decades with their training simulators. For the past 65 years, pilots have had to log hundreds of hours in realistic flight simulators. A main pillar of military and police training is the simulation of dangerous situations.

Now, we're beginning to see simulation training take shape in corporate jobs – where the stakes are far from life-threatening, but still risky in their own way. You know, come to think of it, Walmart on Black Friday actually is a life-threatening situation, which is probably why they are using VR training.

Walmart Leads the Charge

Back in 2017, Walmart with help from the VR company STRIVR, brought VR Training to each of their 200 Walmart Academies for the purpose of management instruction. Satisfied with the results, they announced a month ago that they would bring VR Training to 5,000 stores across the U.S. to improve the training of over 1 million employees. That's a lot of simulations.

This might seem out of character for this seemingly low-tech corporation. However, let's not forget that Walmart is the third largest employer on the face of Earth (behind the US Department of Defense and the People's Liberation Army). Finding ways to optimize their training process is key to Walmart's success.

What's the deal with VR Training?

The clear benefit is that VR offers a hands-on experience very close to the real thing without actually putting a new hire onto the job. It's a way for employees to dip their toes in the water before diving into the shark tank.

Knowledge Anywhere is one particular company that is imagining how VR could be used to train employees in Healthcare, Manufacturing, Technology, Financial, Hospitality, and more. For instance, their President Charlie Gillette gave a presentation on a few different jobs that could benefit from these hands-on experiences.

- Wind turbine maintenance workers – VR could simulate the pressure of repairing turbines at 200 feet tall, with wind blowing in their ears and a lot of open air below them.
- Utility workers – VR could simulate confined areas and possible safety challenges a utility worker may have to assess.
- Sales Reps – it goes without saying the salesmen who learn how to adapt to each scenario are likely to flourish. VR presents limitless scenarios the rep must learn how to adapt to.

These are all positions that could greatly benefit from VR training. But, many of them are at least 3-5 years away from robust applications being created for their disciplines. However, the age of VR training for retail and hospitality is upon us right now – particularly, because of the benefit of special situation management.

Special Situation Management

With Black Friday right around the corner, I'm picturing the absolute chaos that ensues in stores across this nation. VR training could give employees a taste of this situation so they can prepare mentally and physically for how to control these situations.

Additionally, managers can place their future employees in situations that might be rare occurrences but are still important to know how to handle. Like Ryan's interaction with an erratic customer:

> In my year of working as a grocery store cashier back when I was 16, there were only a handful of times where a customer stepped out of line. This one case, there was a man huffing and puffing in the checkout line next to me, clearly agitated that

he had to wait a couple minutes. Out of nowhere, he began shouting rhetorically, but clearly wanting everyone to hear, "I don't understand why you hire all these stupid high schoolers that can't ring up a F****** item to save their life."

Since he was shouting at one of my coworkers, I turned around and told him, "Hey, calm down buddy. She's doing the best she can."

To which he replied, "You better watch your mouth little boy." (Note: this guy was about five-foot nothing. I'm six-foot-five.)

"Little boy? Ha! You're talking to a full-grown man. You need to relax."

A little surprised and embarrassed that I talked back to him, the guy stormed out of the store. Everyone exchanged weird glances wondering what just happened and went on about their business. Five minutes later my manager pulled me into his office and reprimanded me to never step in like that again or he'd have to fire me.

Scenarios like Ryan's arise all the time. Unfortunately, more often for employees of low-wage jobs. They just don't get the respect they deserve. These situations are not easy to handle, especially since the disgruntled customer often takes a jab at the employee's character and self-worth. But it's just something that comes with the territory.

STRIVR is leading the helm of VR training, setting the example for many other industry providers.

By 2024, 90% of the retail and hospitality companies in the Fortune 500 will utilize virtual reality to enhance their employee training.

It goes beyond retail and hospitality positions too.

Preparing for the Worst

What Ryan pointed out with retail, and I'd bet many other people recognize in sales, management, marketing, healthcare, maintenance, etc. is that we're often trained how to work when everything is going smoothly. Training programs may discuss how to handle situations that have gone wrong. But, talking about them is nothing like experiencing them.

Let's take a lesson from the aerospace industry, who use their flight simulators to prepare their pilots for the worst case scenario.

We should be looking to VR training as a way to subject employees to the tough situations that make or break them. Extreme situation management in VR training would do wonders for every single job that involves interpersonal skills, whether this be in sales, nursing, maintenance, etc...

Isn't it ironic to hear that VR will be used in the future to improve our interpersonal skills?

Anyways, this goes to show that when we take VR out of its initial, popular purpose of gaming and entertainment, we'll actually find some quite interesting use cases of how it'll, in fact, improve our lives and make us better social beings. Who knew?

26. Virtual reality might be the next billion-dollar painkiller

> Mind over matter represents the triumph of will over physical hindrance. Our thoughts are our weapon against the world.
> **DAVID ADAM, AUTHOR**

Athletes are all too familiar with this type of advice – that the mind creates all of our boundaries. However, who would've thought that this could be the basis for a new field of medicinal study?

There's a grand idea in the health community known as Virtual Therapeutics, whereby altering a patient's state of mind through multisensory stimulation could act as medicine. Essentially, using virtual reality to make a patient feel less pain and alter their outcomes.

At its most basic level, being the cold-and-flu season, the idea of distracting a child with a VR headset just long enough to give them a flu shot, comes to mind. And while distraction plays a role in lessening pain, researchers are finding ways to go a little deeper into the human psyche:

> The virtual-reality game "Snow World" (a game in which players shoot snowballs to defeat snowman Frosty and his penguins) reportedly works better than morphine at counteracting the pain of patients in burn units.
> **SUSANA MARTINEZ-CONDE**, SCIENTIFIC AMERICAN

It's unbelievable to think that transporting the mind through illusions could be more effective than a painkiller used in every hospital worldwide. Additionally, MRI scans show that playing the game reduces the brain's pain signals. Both mind and matter are impacted.

In all honesty, amplifying the patient experience and brightening their outlook is often times enough to drastically improve patient outcomes. This is the basis for an entire Virtual Therapeutics initiative led by Dr. Brennan Spiegel at Cedars-Sinai:

A YouTube element has been excluded from this version of the text. You can view it online here: https://qtv1.pressbooks.com/?p=277

This is not some rinky-dink, back-alley experiment. This is the official UCLA hospital, running virtual reality experiments with their patients to hopefully determine how the technology can be used to drastically improve healthcare.

Just based on the preliminary experiments of VR affecting patients' perception of pain, I see VR Therapeutics being a crucial tool in treating young patients – who are very susceptible to pain.

By 2033, virtual reality headsets will be commonly found in pediatrician offices nationwide.

However, virtual distraction isn't always the best option for dealing with emotion. On the flip side, VR is shaping up to have a great effect on building our emotional intelligence.

Virtualizing Emotional Intelligence

We're told from a young age to "walk a mile in their shoes" and not judge others before trying to understand where they are coming from. Empathy is a learned skill that a lot of people never take the time to learn. We all know people close to us that never think of the emotions of others before speaking. And it's very hurtful. For this reason, virtual reality could be a groundbreaking platform for turning all those apathetic people around.

Recently, a study found that virtual reality immersion increased people's empathy for one of the most marginalized populations: the homeless. By transporting viewers into the livelihood of a homeless person, the study "led to more positive, longer-lasting attitudes towards the homeless up to two months after the intervention".

Similarly, the use cases for other emotionally charged professions are endless. I can really see therapists and psychiatrists using virtual reality headsets to greatly alter the mindsets of their patients through experiences.

For instance, researchers at Barcelona University are using VR to help people cope with one unavoidable event: death. By putting the viewer in a near-death experience, the experiment has shown to lessen people's fear of death. This would be invaluable to therapy sessions.

Another example of digital therapy comes from Amy Green who created a video game to help people cope with grief, called *The Dragon, Cancer*. It's based on her family's experience when their son, Joel, was given news of terminal cancer. Players are transformed into a witness of Joel's life, exploring an emotional landscape, clicking to discover more of what the family felt and experienced.

It's a hard game to play since it's a game that you can't win. But, it's so much more. As Amy says, "People have to prepare themselves to invest emotionally in a story that they know will break their hearts. But when our hearts break, they heal a little differently."

Virtual Therapeutics is shaping up to be a huge part of healthcare, medicine, and mental health. In fact, Goldman Sachs predicts the market for VR software in the health industry will hit $5.1 billion in sales by 2025.

This is all groundbreaking research and honestly a breath of fresh air.

It shows a side of virtual reality that doesn't involve a user getting lost in a simulated situation and losing sight of reality. These are applications of VR that actually improve the world.

27. An open letter to Magic Leap and the future of augmented reality

> Imagine if the line between the virtual and the real simply didn't exist. Your classroom could become the cosmos. The past could be as vivid as the present. And this is just the beginning. Welcome to a new world.

These are Tim Cook's words about augmented reality. It was a bold claim coming from a company that didn't really have that much skin in the AR game (at the time). They've since created AR Kit, a robust platform for creating mobile AR experiences.

Snapchat's Lens Studio is a really fascinating tool that allows anyone to create AR lenses and same goes for the Facebook AR Suite. But the simple fact is that AR is not meant to be experienced through a phone screen. Honestly, who wants to change the world by looking through their phone's camera lens? It's far too limiting.

This is why Apple won't be the company to take the cake first (although, I still think Tim Cook's statement sums up the possibilities of augmented reality). Most likely, Magic Leap will be the ones to really figure it out.

Why's that?

You might look at their product today, which is ugly and bulky, and think that Magic Leap has no chance. However, Magic Leap has the clearest shot at success because they have created one of the first operating systems native to augmented reality. That is its sole purpose. They could care less how their product looks to a consumer because they aren't trying to sell it to consumers today. They're looking to create the best augmented reality operating system (or Mixed Reality as they like to call it), which then allows for the best experiences to be created.

I was inspired to create this post by the following tweet:

On this day in 2007: Android unveiled

Android market share:

(worldwide*)

2008: 0.5%

2018: 85.9%

(*operating system market share) pic.twitter.com/UYEp0D4PmE

— Jon Erlichman (@JonErlichman) November 5, 2018

Ten years ago, the Android operating system was launched and look what they've done for the world since. I see many similarities between what Android created and the potential of Magic Leap. What follows, are three experiences I'd like Magic Leap developer ecosystem to have achieved within ten years.

Take a Magic Leap... of Faith

To me, Magic Leap's mixed reality glasses fit perfectly in the timeline of the Information Age.

Initially, we got the Internet. Everyone wanted to be digital and create a website. The next great innovation was Internet Search, which made sense out of all these disparate websites. Eventually, this gave way to mobile computing and apps, which maximized the accessibility and uploading of information to the Internet. However, we're at a moment in time where there's an abundance of Information that is being underutilized.

This is where Magic Leap could take us into the next stage of the Information Age, where information is accessible directly to our field of vision via their photonic wafers (basically a lens).

Curiosity Creates Context

A lot of the Internet's information contains spatial qualities. Restaurant reviews are tied to physical locations. Wikipedia pages inform us of historic landmarks beneath our feet; they also bring clarification to the laws of nature around us.

There's an abundance of contextual information passively waiting in our physical surroundings, ready for our curiosity to spike and get us to Google it on our smartphones. Magic Leap brings the process of curiously searching for knowledge directly to our field of view.

> As I write this theory, I'm looking out into an open courtyard, wondering what type of tree is before me with the beautiful ember-colored autumn leaves. Magic Leap (one day) will not only identify what type of tree it is, but also ask me if I'd like to learn why leaves change color – perhaps if I'm interested in hearing a poem by Robert Frost about that particular tree.

As I walk past restaurants, their helpful reviews show up. As I walk past the community center, upcoming classes appear.

If you want to talk about the future of Wikipedia (and the rest of the Internet's information), it's in Magic Leap – helping to bring rich context to our surroundings.

The End of Awkward Silence

When we apply this technology to our interactions with people, theoretically, we'll never again feel at a loss for words. Magic Leap will recognize who's in front of us, scour their social profiles to see what they've been interested in or up to recently and give us something to talk about.

> I don't know about you, but I always feel terrible when I've completely missed a big event in someone's life. Just recently, I found out one of my old college friend's got offered a job with the Milwaukee Bucks. A dream come true for him. Days earlier I was talking with him and didn't congratulate him because I didn't know. Somehow, that life update passed right by me. And here I am, weeks after the big day, sending him a congratulations.
> RYAN, INEVITABLE/HUMAN

Sometimes all we need is a small talking point to get a conversation going. Magic Leap offers an opportunity where we truly become more social because of our technology.

Speaking of social moments...

Layers of Time

Each and every photograph we take with our phones is geotagged. Meaning, there's a GPS coordinate encoded in that photograph (unless you explicitly turn it off). Although this rarely proves to be useful to us, it presents an interesting new experience in Magic Leap.

Photographs could in a way act as digital graffiti, recorded in the place they were taken, and viewable through our Magic Leap glasses at a later date. As you walk by different locations, photographs that were once taken there could be viewed.

There would be different sharing settings, of course, controlling whether or not your photo is public and whose photos you want to be able to view. Perhaps you are going for total publicity. Maybe you'd prefer just family and friends in those locations.

Imagine traveling to Paris, standing in the same spot your mother and father took a picture, seeing that photo, and taking your own. It's kind of like leaving photographic breadcrumbs in places you've traveled. Who knows, one day it could turn into an entirely new travel experience for future generations to walk the same paths as their ancestors.

This would also be fascinating for landscape photography. I, for one, love walking past big construction projects to watch their progress over time. However, by the time the new building has gone up, I've forgotten what it used to look like.

> The Rodney Dangerfield movie *Back to School,* takes place at the University of Wisconsin – Madison. In a way, the movie acts as a geographic time capsule for all the buildings at the time of shooting over 30 years ago.

Looking at old pictures or videos somewhat fills this curiosity. But, imagine your field of vision incorporating pictures from the past for comparison with the real thing today.

In a way, we'd be layering moments in time – effectively time traveling to a location's past.

Naturally, there are a number of possible advances that augmented and mixed reality could bring to the world. That's why it is so exciting.

However, the greatest value AR has to offer is bringing context to our surroundings – feeding us information about the current situation that can inform us to make better decisions, recognize opportunities, and be more aware of our surroundings?

28. The innovation that'll take us from New York to London in 30 minutes

I'm at the airport multiple times a month. Cutting travel time in half is a huge deal for me. The time saved compounds into days. That's why I use Clear, which is cutting the time surrounding travel – eliminating security lines, bag-checking, and waiting at the terminal.

However, Clear isn't the only innovation we're striving for in aviation. What peaks my interest are scramjets shooting us through the atmosphere at 6,000mph. Now that's something that has my imagination running wild.

What the heck is a scramjet? Take NASA's word for it:

> **One thing has always been true about rockets: The farther and faster you want to go, the bigger your rocket needs to be.**
>
> **Why? Rockets combine a liquid fuel with liquid oxygen to create thrust. Take away the need for liquid oxygen and your spacecraft can be smaller or carry more payload.**
>
> **That's the idea behind a different propulsion system called "scramjet," or Supersonic Combustion Ramjet: The oxygen needed by the engine to combust is taken from the atmosphere passing through the vehicle, instead of from a tank onboard. The craft becomes smaller, lighter and faster.**

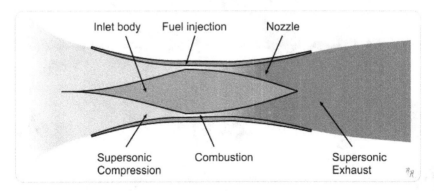

Inlet body   Fuel injection   Nozzle

Supersonic Compression   Combustion   Supersonic Exhaust

It's unbelievable how simple the design of a scramjet is. The fact that they could propel you to 7,000mph seems practically alien. Why are we not using scramjets for travel?

Well, the aircraft needs to be traveling at roughly Mach 6 (six times the speed of sound) before the air traveling through the scramjet compresses enough to balance with the fuel injection. It's why they've actually been labeled as "air-breathing engines".

This means you either need to launch a scramjet off of a high-powered rocket. Or dropped from an aircraft traveling at sufficient speed, which is how NASA launched their X-43A Scramjet (awesome video of scramjet reaching Mach 7).

Granted, this was back in 2004 that NASA launched the first scramjet and they would soon thereafter up the ante to Mach 10 (nearly 7,000mph). In other words, a flight from NYC to London would take just 30 minutes.

In reality, this invention will exist for the sole purpose of governments and militaries for quite some time. And the fact we haven't heard much about scramjets since 2004, tells me that they're serving that purpose now.

But, that can't stop us from imagining scramjets screaming through our atmosphere. In fact, NASA even put together design prototypes of what commercial scramjets might one day look like.

Nonetheless, there's really one thing I'd like to leave you with:

- We entered the 19th century at 6mph (horse-drawn carriage)
- We entered the 20th century at 60mph (steam-powered locomotive)
- We entered the 21st century at 600mph (intercontinental airplane)

Will we enter the 22nd century traveling at 6,000 mph?

29. Will you surf the Internet of DNA?

The internet is an invention of connection. Connecting information. Connecting products. Connecting people. But can it sustain a more meaningful connection – connecting genetic information?

If so, then we're on the cusp of massive medical breakthrough – from curing rare diseases to understanding the pathways of mental illness. The time for the Internet of DNA is upon us. Especially since genomic testing has taken off in the last few years:

> **The largest labs can now sequence human genomes to a high polish at the pace of two per hour. The first genome took about 13 years... DNA sequencing will be capable of producing 85 petabytes of data this year worldwide. For comparison, all the master copies of movies held by Netflix take up 2.6 petabytes of storage.**
> **ANTONIO REGALADO,** MIT TECHNOLOGY REVIEW

All of this DNA information is relatively useless if it can't be accessed asynchronously by doctors, researchers, and consumers. Similar to how Wikipedia relinquished us from the barrier to knowledge.

The biggest benefit of an Internet of DNA is what's called genetic matchmaking. Essentially, this is the concept that specific sequences of DNA that cause disease, illness, etc. are common among other patients suffering from the same problem. This would allow doctors to learn from the practices of others before.

For instance, this could be invaluable for cancer treatment. Tumors are the result of genetic mutations. Doctors that can match similar mutations to previous cancer patients, effectively unlock insight into a smoother treatment – what medication worked, for what period of time, etc. Similarly, this could be the key to solving rare diseases that affect less than a thousand people worldwide.

Scientists think they'll need to sort through a million genomes

or more to solve cases that could involve a single rogue DNA letter, or to make discoveries about the genetics of common diseases that involve a complex combination of genes.
ANTONIO REGALADO, MIT TECHNOLOGY REVIEW

Preliminary editions of the Internet of DNA are Matchmaker Exchange and WuXi NextCODE. Both of them are still challenged by bringing a useful amount of data onto the exchange while ensuring that the database is easy to search and utilize for all parties (not just researchers).

It's not until 2025 that we'll see the first iteration of a consumer-facing Internet of DNA.

A consumer-facing Internet of DNA is interesting because it would allow for connection on a new level. It's always nice to meet someone in the same boat as you, especially when things go awry. Yes, there are cancer support groups and alcoholism support groups. But, to meet one or two other people that have the exact same genetic source to the problem as you, well that seems extra comforting.

The fact of the matter is that the Internet of DNA could be an entirely new version of communication – where you connect with like-minded and "like-gened people.

Will you surf the Internet of DNA?

30. Will Big Data create an entirely new NFL?

In light of the NFL season opener tomorrow night, I thought it'd be interesting to ponder technology's role in football. Not today. In 2028.

Historically, the NFL is slow to adopt tech. They banned in-helmet microphones for 40 years. And even now, it comes with a slew of rules.

The NFL is slow to adopt tech because they fear it could jeopardize the integrity of the sport. Any change must improve the game, work reliably, and it cannot favor one team over another.

This is why I struggle to see the NFL ever implementing the GoRout Heads-Up Display (HUD) in helmets. But it's a possibility, nonetheless. Similar to how fighter pilots have a lot of their data and readings displayed digitally on their visor, GoRout imagines a helmet visor that displays play calls and other information. In other words, it's an augmented reality display for players.

Today, the product is designed for the practice field only. By 2028, though, this could be more along the lines of an Iron-Man-like display. I imagine a play going like so:

- The quarterback is under center, analyzing the field. His HUD takes into account the stances of linebackers and the secondary, suggesting which ones are going to blitz. He's then given the optimal audible to call – a running play.

- The running back takes the hand-off and instantly his HUD updates to show which gap is the likeliest to open up based on an analysis of all his blockers. He hits that gap and breaks one out to the sideline.
- The wide receiver, who is now blocking downfield to extend the run, sees in the corner of his HUD a real-time video from the running back's point-of-view – thus the wide receiver knows which way to block. He moves his body between the cornerback and running back and the running back breaks one 65-yards for a touchdown.

This is just an example scenario from the Offense's perspective where a Heads-Up Display could be invaluable to their strategy. Let's not forget that the Defense has access to the same tools and will likely be using it to throw off the Offense. **Ironically, the introduction of computers to football will actually make game strategy more complex.**

The defining factor for this to become a reality in ten years is DATA. After one week of games, the NFL (in conjunction with Amazon's Next Gen Stats platform) receives nearly 3TB of data which it distributes to teams. But this is all after-the-fact.

For HUDs to become a piece of equipment on every player's head, the data must become real-time. The average NFL play lasts just 4 seconds. This means **data must be collected, sorted, and analyzed... then turned into actionable insights and displayed in the player's interface in fractions of seconds.** If any hiccup happens along the way, if even one second of buffering occurs, the play has passed and the data is useless. In other words, this is a huge challenge for computer scientists.

Also, let's remember that the NFL's guidelines for tech usage are extremely stringent. For instance, if one sideline's microphone communication with their quarterback stops working, then the other team is required to stop using theirs.

Nonetheless, Amazon is getting their reps in with the Next Gen Stats program (interesting video). By placing RFID chips in the shoulder pads of every player, they're able to track each player's movement patterns and turn it into insight – this is where the 3TB of data comes from.

The Next Gen Stats program over the next five years aims to impact the game in three ways:

- Evaluating player performance during games.
- Providing analysts, broadcasters, and announcers with data to break downplays and add insight for the viewer.
- Introduce novel statistics to fantasy sports and dedicated fans.

If the program exceeds expectations, are then I'm sure that the NFL will continue to call upon Amazon to modernize the technology present in the sport. Maybe someday they'll even bring Amazon Alexa (a more advanced version than today of course) into the helmet of every player.

Anyways, no fan wants to see football become a computer vs. computer sport, losing its nuances and turning players into puppets. Yet, we also don't want to see football fall behind the times. The solution: methodically utilize some of the cool instruments that technology has to offer. Who knows, we might just mess around and create a better sport.

Will Big Data create an entirely new NFL?